Our Trees

By buying this book you also bought the right to get a tree planted.

Go to **www.pinetribe.com/planting** to claim your tree.

Going digital is good for the reader, good for the author and good for the planet. That's why at Pine Tribe we only deliver digital books and print-on-demand to minimise waste. But that's just the start of our quest. We plant lots of trees. We just love trees. Maybe you do too.

THOMAS FLINDT

HAPPY LEMONS
How Laughter Breeds Success

Happy Lemons - How Laughter Breeds Success
© Thomas Flindt and Pine Tribe Ltd. 2014

Ghostwriter: Julia Hilliard
Editors: Julia Hilliard and Kalimaya Krabbe
Cover design and typesetting: Patricia Hepe
Photographs: Kirsten Fich
Photo credits (cover): Lars Schmidt *www.schmidtaps.com*
1st edition 2014

ISBN: 978-0-9912609-8-0

www.pinetribe.com/thomas-flindt

Pine Tribe Ltd.
International House
1 St Katharine's Way
London, E1W 1UN

TABLE OF CONTENTS

INTRODUCTION:
    Then the laughter started
    - The story of the Four Systems Experiment   7

CHAPTER 1:
    Why laughter is good for you   18

CHAPTER 2:
    The history of laughter   24

CHAPTER 3:
    Group laughter in your living room   33

CHAPTER 4:
    Why we laugh   42

CHAPTER 5:
    How you can use laughter to breed success   100

EXERCISES   121

REFERENCES   124

Only a person who risks is free

To laugh is to risk appearing the fool.
To weep is to risk appearing sentimental.
To reach for another is to risk involvement.
To expose your feelings is to risk exposing your true self.
To place your ideas, your dreams, before a crowd
is to risk their loss.
To love is to risk not being loved in return.
To live is to risk dying.
To believe is to risk despair.
To try is to risk failure.
But risks must be taken, because the greatest
hazard in life is to risk nothing.
The person who risks nothing, has nothing, is nothing.
They may avoid suffering and sorrow, but they cannot
learn, feel, change, grow, love, live.
Chained by their attitudes they are slaves; they have
forfeited their freedom.
Only a person who risks is free.

- Hugo Prather

INTRODUCTION

Then the laughter started - The story of the Four Systems Experiment

I've been working with laughter for more than ten years now. After a year working with laughter, I felt that it had made such an enormous difference to my life, and that it could make such an enormous difference to other people's lives, that the time had come for me to document some of the facts and claims that I based my lectures on.

I had been telling my audiences that laughter was the best remedy for stress, and how we create contact with the present moment and each other when we laugh together. I had described how laughter makes us 'fit for fight', more motivated and receptive, and how a good laugh can neutralise narratives that belong to the past and future, allowing us to see each other as we are, right now.

I had often said that being able to have a good laugh together improves communication and cooperation between people. However, it is one thing to have read about these theories, it is another thing to be able to talk about them from the perspective of your own documented experience.

I made a decision to find a company that I could work with for an extended period of time. My idea was this: to start every working day with 10-20 minutes of laughter for all the company's employees. Over the course of a month, we would measure how the health of the company and the employees could be improved through the practice of laughter. I was certain that it would be a major success.

At my next presentation I shared my plans to scientifically document the beneficial effects my group were feeling and the fact that I was looking for a business with which to work on this experiment. A man I would come to know as Christoffer Witt Quist instantly raised his hand and said, "Count us in!". Christoffer was the director and owner of an IT firm near Copenhagen, Denmark, called Four Systems. I left the bright smiles and appreciative applause of this happy gathering. It was dark outside in the parking lot, but the night sky was perfectly clear and filled with stars. I stood for a moment and looked up at the stars. They spoke their own language. I had this powerful intuition that this - with Christoffer's card in my pocket - was the start of something big.

How laughter changed my life

I've spent a decade helping people use laughter to change their lives, so it makes sense that I tell you where it all began, and how laughter changed my life.

I grew up in a wonderful happy family, in a town just north of Copenhagen. My father, a man I admire a great deal, ran a supermarket. When I grew up, I followed in his footsteps and trained as a grocer. Deep down, I knew that this wasn't the right thing for me so as the years passed I became unhappier and unhappier, and angrier and more bitter, until I received the most incredible gift – I got fired!

I went back to school, and felt my creativity start to unfurl and flourish as I began painting and writing poetry. I was lucky to have an incredibly inspirational mentor, the language teacher, writer and Marilyn Monroe expert, Bo Tao Michaelis. His artistic and entertaining style of teaching (which he called "Tao's Total Show") helped awaken my own desire to communicate and to teach.

Inspired by his example, I trained as a teacher, and after some years studying the theory and practice of human development (at university and in the classroom with my students!) I decided to take what I had learned and use it for the education and enlightenment of adults. At a training session one day, I happened upon a laughter workshop. In that hour, I experienced all the values I wished for in life, and all those I wanted to share with others, coming to me one by one, like pearls threaded on a string, through an intense immersion in laughter. I felt a vivid presence and awareness within myself, and a great love for myself and for those laughing with me. I experienced a deep contact with life itself. I experienced true freedom.

There is a sense of magic in laughter, and I knew my life had been touched by it. I knew that I had encountered something incredibly special, and that I had to share it with everyone. Not long after that, I handed in my notice as a teacher and devoted myself to the path of laughter.

Morning laughter

- With the cooperation of Four Systems, I planned to measure the mental and physical rewards of starting the day with 10-20 minutes of laughter.

- How would it affect each individual worker and what would it mean for cooperation, communication and social relations in the workplace?

- How would it influence the company in the long term?

- Would starting each morning in this way influence the rest of the working day?

And would 10-20 minutes of morning laughter perhaps affect the working environment in other ways?

In April 2004, I held an introductory evening for all of the Four Systems employees. They gave the project the thumbs up, agreeing to laugh together every working day throughout the month of May. Before we started, all the employees were asked to fill out a questionnaire about their physical and psychological working environment. They responded to questions about cooperation and communication, quality of social relations and level of personal wellbeing, and made evaluations of the workplace as a whole.

Stress test

Prior to the start of our course, stress researcher Anders Lonedahl, from the Karolinska Institute in Stockholm, Sweden, visited the company. I had met Anders earlier that year in a completely different context, where I had happened to mention my idea and he had expressed his interest in becoming involved. Lonedahl came to Four Systems early in the morning on May 3rd and stress-tested four randomly selected employees.

Lonedahl measured their blood pressure, pulse and carbon dioxide (CO_2) exhalation levels. When we are stressed, we accumulate CO_2 in the body and the levels of it that we exhale decrease. All four employees tested as having too high a pulse rate and blood pressure, and too low a level of exhaled CO_2. Psychological testing revealed that all four were exhibiting stress behaviour. Every morning for the next four weeks, all the employees were going to laugh with me for 10-20 minutes. Apart from the laughing itself, the sessions would also include stretching and breathing exercises and always finished off with a silent meditation or massage.

Then the laughter started. We met every morning at 8:30 a.m. at exactly the same spot – an area of carpet just in front of the company's canteen. After a few days, something exciting started to happen.

I noted in my log book that on day 4, several employees actually began to laugh at 8:28 a.m. as they were walking onto the carpeted area. In other words, they started to laugh *before* we began the laughter session. Had the bodies of these people acquired a form of inner 'laughter clock' which had now been programmed to start ticking at 8:30 a.m.? It was as if their bodies knew that it was time to laugh. Or had the 'laughing spot' here in front of the canteen accumulated so many positive associations, that one only had to step into the area for the laughter to begin? For me, this was a very exciting observation and it was refreshing and life-affirming to be met each morning by such laughing, bright faces.

Laughing fit

On the 10th day, the workers told me that the effects of their morning laughter had now become tangible throughout the entire workplace. The morning ritual was helping people to be more authentic and more prone to laughter during the working day. I was told that spontaneous outbursts of uncontrollable laughter had become a more regular event at Four Systems. Sometimes, just a glance from a colleague would start off a fit of laughter. Whenever anything funny happened at work, people would allow themselves to laugh and enjoy it, rather than hurry themselves along. It had become more natural and more legitimate to laugh in the workplace.

After three weeks, one of the company's bookkeepers, Jane Dixen, made a bet with her boss. She bet a kilo of candy that she could sit through the next laughter session without laughing. This wasn't because Jane didn't like laughing, but purely to test herself. Jane was certain that she could sit amongst us for the whole session and refrain from laughing. A whole kilo of candy was at stake. Jane managed to sit stony-faced for around 45 seconds in the free laughter session before totally collapsing into laugher.

I thought it was an amazing experiment. Jane experienced that she had no control in this situation, that laughter isn't something you just hold back. Of course, I will never know to what extent Jane attempted to fight the impulse to laugh, but at least this tells me that a good laugh is worth far more than a kilo of candy!

After four weeks of laughter sessions at Four Systems, stress researcher Anders Lonedahl dropped by again. The same four test subjects had their pulse, blood pressure and CO_2 exhalation levels measured again. The results were exciting. Three out of four of these individuals were no longer showing signs of stress behaviour. Three out of four now had normal pulse, blood pressure and CO_2 exhalation levels. A very satisfactory result for both myself and Four Systems.

Report by stress researcher Anders Lonedahl, Karolinska Institute, Stockholm, Sweden.

"In conditions of stress, the body's 'fight or flight' system is activated. We begin to breathe more rapidly and CO_2 levels in exhaled breath decrease immediately. The body's muscles become tense and our pulse rate rises. The blood is directed away from peripheral areas of the body such as the hands, feet and skin.

Digestion is put on hold. Functioning of the immune system is initially enhanced but in cases of longer periods of stress, it becomes depleted. Creativity wanes. Reproductive capability is decreased.

The purpose of the 'fight or flight' reaction is to enable us to survive a life-threatening event - a stress response which we share with all other mammals. However, in modern society, we seldom encounter life-threatening situations. Yet our brains react to everyday stress in the same way - as if we had met a huge bear! We can't always react in the way our biological systems would like us to though. We stay seated in our meeting even though we would rather attack the chairperson or run, screaming, out of the door.

The test that we carried out at Four Systems shows the positive effects that laughter has on stress levels in the body. The results of participating were fantastic! Wellbeing has improved and the social atmosphere has become much better within the group. Stress levels have fallen drastically at Four Systems and great steps forward have been taken in terms of the psychological working environment.

A workplace evaluation was repeated and the results were striking. All the employees showed a substantial improvement in evaluations of their work, themselves and their colleagues".

What the workers thought

Here are a few extracts from some of the workplace evaluations taken after the course of morning laughter:

Going to work has become much more fun. We are allowed to enjoy ourselves at work now. We laugh much more with each other than we ever did before.

Personally, I now have more energy and greater levels of mental resources. I have noticed that there is a stronger feeling of solidarity and cohesiveness in the workplace.
 - *Anne von Haven Theilade, Bookkeeper*

I see things more positively now. It feels as though I have more resources at my disposal. I think my colleagues are happier. The morning laughter sessions have contributed to giving us a better working environment.

- Steen Bagger Carstensen, Account Manager

I think the boss is happier. It seems like he has opened up more and has become more positive.

- Helle Lausch, Account Manager

It has become a far more enjoyable place to work in. The atmosphere is really good now. We laugh together more than we did before. I feel less stressed than before. I notice that I have acquired much more energy.

- Christoffer Witt Quist, Company Director

In May 2004, the turnover at Four Systems increased by 34% (compared to figures in May 2003). May 2004 was one of the most exciting months of my life. I had been given the opportunity to try out all my theory and knowledge in practice. I had been present throughout the entire process and had experienced first-hand the body's capacity for invisible communication. Together with the employees at Four Systems, I had been able to speak laughter's loving, intimate and egalitarian language for an entire month. With laughter, we had opened up doors, windows, eyes, ears and hearts. We had experienced something quite special that month. I could feel that I had become close to several of the company's workers and it was with considerable sadness that I said goodbye.

The Four Systems experiment turned out to be a gigantic success and was covered widely by the Danish media. The laughing colleagues were featured on several national TV stations and in numerous newspapers. I was especially pleased with the headline on the cover of Computerworld (Denmark's leading computer magazine), "IT company laughs profits up".

In August of the same year, just as I was thinking Four Systems was a completed chapter of my life, my mobile rang.

- "Hi Thomas – this is Christoffer Quist here - how's it going?"

- "Fine thanks, how's it going with you guys?" I answered.
- "Very well, thanks. I've just employed some more staff here at Four Systems", he continued. "You know, I have to tell you, the others keep asking about you. So, I thought that perhaps we could arrange an extra 14 days of morning laughter. What do you say?"

I thought a little and answered, "14 days of morning laughter is a very short-term solution. Why not a more permanent solution? What about laughing every Monday morning for as long as you feel like it… half a year, maybe even a whole year?"

- "Great", answered Christoffer, "You've got a deal!"

On World Laughter Day 2005, the pioneer of laughter yoga Madan Kataria presented that year's Business Laughter Prize to Four Systems. The computer company had, by this time, laughed every Monday morning for the entire year. Today, Four Systems[1] serves as a shining example to the fact that joy and happiness are not just reserved for our private lives. It should be good fun, even a celebration, to go to work. Having fun in the workplace is not lazy or fickle. Laughter is an energy that lifts us up and releases creativity, cooperation and growth. Laughter gives us energy and motivates us. The accounts at Four Systems convey this message clearly: in the period May 2004 to May 2005, the company's turnover increased by 0% (compared to the previous year).

In this book, my aim is to inspire you to find your original source of deep and authentic laughter – your laughing self. This is the laughter you were born with, the laughter that is truly you; the state where you laugh freely without worries, where you allow yourself full expression as a person.

This book will take you through the steps that will lead you to a better, more enjoyable and meaningful life. A life in which happiness is a tangible presence and where you decide which direction your life will take. A life where you grow and develop continually, and in so doing, increase the levels of resources available to yourself and to others.

To be in a state of constant development, working towards greater and greater levels of happiness, affects everything you do – both your actions and your words. In this way, you also motivate and teach others to grow. When we are able to help each other to grow positively, we can create a world in which each of us flourishes and is cherished. It is through the door of your laughter that you can access your innermost essence. You can get in touch with your reality - your true and authentic self. Through your laughter, you can learn to achieve your fullest potential as a human being.

When we laugh, we release tension and stress. When we laugh we let go of ego. When we laugh, we experience states of harmony, happiness and balance. We come into contact with ourselves, and with life itself. Happiness and bliss are tangible when we laugh. Within laughter and behind laughter is the secret of you and your inner joy. In this book, I will describe the conditions that can lead you to experience greater joy and a happier life. Happiness can never be a constant state – if it were, we would not recognise or be aware of the feeling as it arose – but you can bring more happiness, laughter and success into your life. The secret is within you and within the pages of this book!

CHAPTER #1

1
Why laughter is good for you

In 1995, a medical doctor named Madan Kataria sat down to write an article about laughter for a medical journal in India. He had decided to investigate and describe the physiological changes that laughter causes in the body. The more he researched this topic, the more his enthusiasm grew, as it seemed that laughter had a healing, protective and strengthening effect upon the entire human physiology. It looked like laughter was just about the best medicine this doctor had ever stumbled upon in his entire 20-year career!

Today it is a well-documented fact that laughter has a preventative and healing effect on our physiological condition. Here are some of the documented effects of laughter[2]:

- Laughter strengthens the circulatory, respiratory and digestive systems.
- Laughter leads to the release of the hormones dopamine, serotonin and oxytocin (sometimes known as the "cuddle

hormone") as well as endorphins; the body's own mood elevators and painkillers.
- Laughter lowers the levels of stress hormones in your blood.
- Laughter increases lung capacity and oxygen content of the blood.
- Laughter causes us to burn more calories.
- 10 minutes of laughter has the same effect on the heart and lungs as half an hour of light jogging.
- 10 minutes of laughter releases the same amount of endorphins as 20 minutes of sex or 30 minutes of jogging.
- 10 minutes of laughter can cause our blood pressure to fall by up to 15%. For the same reason, laughter has a positive effect on cardiovascular and respiratory disease.
- Laughter increases blood flow to your muscles and internal organs and stimulates organ function.
- Laughter leads to an increase in the number of white blood cells available to fight disease and boosts immune response.
- Laughter helps us to recover more rapidly from illness.
- Laughter appears to have a positive effect on up to 70% of the health problems most common to the Western world!

For many years now, laughter has been the subject of scientific research studies, and there can be no doubt of the positive value of a good belly-laugh. Research has even shown that simulated laughter has the same effect on the body as genuine laughter!

Don't forget that in our experiment at Four Systems in May 2004, we also clearly demonstrated that laughter helps our health by reducing stress levels, giving us more coping resources, enabling us to see things more positively, and giving us more energy.

Another famous doctor who understands the power of laughter is Patch Adams. Hunter Doherty "Patch" Adams suffered from depression as a young man, and after making several suicide attempts, he decided instead to work to change the world. He dedicated himself to serving other people, trying to create a revolution of love and kindness. While at medical school he realised that the way medicine was practised was humourless, hierarchical and unfair. He found that humour is a painkiller, prevents burnout, and creates a cooperative environment, and so resolved to spend his life working to create happy hospitals. His whole career has been dedicated to creating a holistic type of medicine which treats patients as people and not a collection of symptoms. He founded the Gesundheit Institute in 1971, where they offered free holistic (conventional and complementary) medical care to patients for a period of 12 years. And now, takes groups of clowns around the world, including into war zones and refugee camps, because he says that "clowning [is] a trick to get love close[3]." They also build schools and clinics at some of the sites they visit. Patch has said: "If you want to be well, be happy! And have an exercise programme[4]."

Letting go and opening up

> We have let go of the belief that we must be normal. It robs us of the possibility to be extraordinary and leads us to mediocrity.
> - Uta Hagen

Laughter opens us like nothing else: we extend our chests forward, throw our arms back and open our mouths wide. Our faces and bodies become completely open when we laugh and this physiological unfolding influences our mental state. The behaviour of the body affects the workings of the mind, and vice versa. If we maintain this state of bodily and facial openness longer than we normally do, then the mind is reminded of how liberating and beneficial it is to open up in this way, and it becomes trained to repeat such an experience. When we allow our bodies to unfold and the laughter to roll through us, we come into contact with our truth and sincerity. During a fit of laughter, the brain totally lets go and you get an opportunity to see yourself and your life as it truly is, here and now. When you laugh, you lose control for a short while. The very experience of being able to let go is unbelievably liberating.

When we laugh, we fill the room and make ourselves heard. The face and the body change form and expression during this process. This experience can be a very unfamiliar one for some group laughter participants. For example, the Danes are a lovely race. We are decent people. We are known for being among the friendliest people in the world. But this tendency towards friendliness can also be a bit too much and can even take the pleasure out of our interactions with others. Being friendly people, we just don't want to offend anyone. Many Danes have been raised to mind their manners and to regulate themselves - both in terms of sound and expression. Don't make a spectacle of yourself! Laughter can disturb other people, so don't enjoy life too much, you might bother someone in the process! And yes, if you are a Dane, you have probably found yourself being firmly put in place by the invisible *Jante's law* (I'll tell you more about this in Chapter 4) on countless occasions over the years, so it has become easier for you to hide your light under a bushel rather than come out and show what you are really made of.

In countries like the UK and the US it seems you have the opposite problem. Margaret Thatcher told you in 1987 that "there is no such thing as society. There are individual men and women, and there are families." You've been told that greed is good, that individualism is the most important thing and that everyone should look out only for themselves. However, laughter can give all of us what we need. In the same way that laughter can help us find our own individual nature and expression in a society that emphasises collectivity, laughter can also help us connect with each other and form stronger communities in a society that focuses on individualism. (We saw this in the Four Systems experiment, where the workers felt that laughter had helped improve solidarity and cohesiveness among the workforce.)

Laughing together fosters a sense of community and connection, which we all need not only to flourish, but to survive! Robert Putnam, author of "Bowling Alone" states that joining and participating in just one group cuts your odds of dying next year in half[5]. Bowling Alone is a study based on nearly 500,000 interviews with Americans, which examines the collapse and revival of the American community.

Similar studies in the UK have also found a link between social cohesion and improved health in communities.

Whichever direction 'fitting in' takes you, many people place restraining orders on themselves in order to 'fit in'. I must ask you, what is it that you need to 'fit in' with? Do you need to 'fit in' with all those people who don't really know how to enjoy life? Do you need to 'fit in' with all those who don't give expression to the life force that flows through them? Do you want to live up to an image that perhaps has nothing to do with reality? (What you think others are thinking about you may well just be an illusion).

Others stop themselves from laughing so as not to be seen by others. If you happen to be shy by nature, this is nothing to be ashamed of, but if you resist your laughter because you are worried about what others might think, then do your best to change this way of thinking as soon as possible. The others are looking at you because they are curious – deep down, everyone loves the sound of happy laughter.

When we laugh, we activate bodily and expressive states which we may have suppressed for many years. Through laughter, we embark on an inner and outer journey - both physiologically and mentally. The inner journey is that of freeing yourself through laughter. Your inner laugh, your vibrant laughing self, suddenly comes to life. Laughter can activate your slumbering creativity and gives birth to new forms within you. You come into contact with your spontaneity and a deep, original form of expression that lives within you. You will notice how satisfied, relieved and free of worries you become when you step into this state.

Laughter loosens up those psychological bonds that have inhibited or restrained your happiness over the years. This is the key to freeing an abundant source of uninhibited, carefree hilarity, for much of our laughter lies hidden in our very understanding of ourselves. We have been raised and educated with certain assumptions regarding how we should behave and how we should be. We even have specific images or ideas of how we should look. Many people are captives of this image, not allowing themselves the freedom of their own unique expression, but rather straining to maintain the particular image they have ascribed themselves.

You can laugh your way to health and happiness!

CHAPTER #2

2
The history of laughter

The prehistoric roots of laughter – or why laughter is infectious

In December 2006, it was scientifically proven that laughter is infectious, when a group of researchers at University College London published results demonstrating how and why we are so affected by the sound of laughter. An area of the brain called the pre-motor cortex controls our facial muscles, including the smile response. This area is directly stimulated by sounds of laughter or whoops of joy. One million years ago, when we were still living in caves, this part of the brain developed with the purpose of ensuring group adaptation and social assimilation. We used laughter as a signal, a way of communicating that we were a part of the tribe. So when members of the group laughed everyone in the group laughed along with them - to signal community and solidarity.

Some scientists think that laughter was even a precursor to language and that humans laughed before we could even speak since the neural circuits for laughter exist in such ancient regions of the brain, and some of our animal cousins (including chimpanzees, one of our closest relatives) show laughter-like sounds when playing[7], and contagious, responsive laughter behaviour. The deep evolutionary basis of laughter shows that it must have provided our ape ancestors with a social advantage[8].

In 1962 in a small village called Kashasha, in what is now Tanzania, a laughter epidemic began with three girls at a boarding school and raced through the school until it had to be temporarily closed! The laughter then spread to a nearby village and another nearby school. All in all, around 1000 people were affected, and 14 schools had to be closed during the epidemic[9]. Sadly, this laughing outbreak was more likely due to mass hysteria than happiness or humour!

Throughout the decade I have spent working with laughter, I have seen, heard and felt many insanely funny and infectious ways of laughing. A few years ago, I gathered together 20 very unique people who had this particular talent in common – a very special and very infectious laugh. We went to a recording studio and made a CD of Denmark's funniest and most inspiring laughter. All with one purpose: to help you and the rest of the world have a really good laugh! You can purchase *Greatest Laughter Volume 1* from www.pinetribe.com/thomas-flindt/greatest-laughs

Laughter in the east

For thousands of years, the conscious use of laughter as communication has been practised in the Far East. Buddhist monks, striving to live in the present moment, have used laughter to purify their minds. Long before the first scientific trials were ever conducted on laughter, these monks knew that when we speak, we create tension in our mind that removes us from the present moment. Therefore, by laughing intentionally after each sentence they spoke, these monks found that they could release this tension and cleanse themselves mentally. Letting go of the control that arises in a conversation. Try and imagine how funny a conversation like this could be....

Exercise: Laugh like a monk
Try it yourself!

One evening, when you are in the company of good friends, tell your friends the story of the Buddhist monks that finish off each sentence with a chuckle or a giggle. Explain also why they do this. Make an agreement with your friends that for the next hour, they should laugh every time they utter a sentence. It doesn't matter if you talk about politics, science or personal relationships. The subject is not important; the rule is just to laugh every time you say a sentence.

Smiling can also relax you and help you to deal with stress. Scientists at the University of Kansas conducted a study about the effect of smiling on stress by getting study participants to hold a chopstick in their mouth in a way which stimulated the main "smiling muscles" while other participants held a neutral facial expression. Participants were then asked to complete test activities designed to be stressful. The people who smiled during the stressful test activities had lower recovery heart rates after the activities were completed.

This means that smiling during a stressful activity can help reduce the intensity of your stress response, whether or not you feel happy while you're doing it. It turns out there is truth to the phrase "Grin and bear it[10]"!

The origins of the laughter club

Laughter yoga, or group laughter, is only in its infancy – it has only existed for about two decades. The Indian doctor, Madan Kataria, had the idea, drawing on a combination of Eastern philosophy and modern Western science. As he wrote his article on laughter for a medical journal, he was so overwhelmed by the potential of what he was writing that it kept him awake all night. And so it happened that at 4 a.m. on

March 13th 1995, in the Indian town of Mumbai, a new idea was born. If laughter is the best medicine we have, then obviously we need to have a place where people can go and laugh. This is how the seeds of the first laughter club were sown. That very same morning, three hours later, Madan Kataria went out to the local park in Mumbai and told some people about his idea. At first these early-risers thought the doctor had lost his marbles, but when he began to explain his idea along with all the scientific facts he had learned about laughter, people began to sit up and take notice. By 7 a.m. the world's first laughter club had become a reality.

They formed a circle, and the town's funniest men and women were placed at the centre of this circle. Everyone there told jokes of all kinds but not all were told with equal success. The quality of the humour was wide-ranging and only a few people actually laughed as much as the doctor had hoped. After 10 days, there were no more jokes to draw upon. The jokes started getting dirty, not everyone was happy about that. Some of the people present said that if this was the only way to create laughter, then they just didn't want to participate. After two weeks, the project had reached a dead end.

However, Dr. Kataria was so convinced that his idea could work that he continued to study and read about laughter. Both the most up-to-date research and the most ancient of historical knowledge about the power of laughter came under the doctor's scrutiny. He came upon descriptions of a form of 'laughter meditation' that had been used many years ago within certain schools of yoga. In this 'laughter meditation', laughter was facilitated collectively without relying on jokes or humour. The idea was to let the laughter arise from within and to use this laughter to open up both body and mind, creating a bridge to the present moment and thus an alternative route to happiness. Bingo!

Shortly afterwards, Doctor Kataria devised the first ever laughter exercises. The doctor's idea went under the slogan of *'simulated stimulated laughter'*. 'Simulated' because we start the laughter process ourselves and 'stimulated' because all of our internal organs are stimulated by this action. Laughter yoga had now found a form and since then has spread like wildfire around the globe with 4000 known laughter clubs now in existence. Thank you Madan! You can laugh in clubs from Sydney, Australia to Kingston, Jamaica. There are laughter clubs in Paris, London and New York – you name it and you can laugh there. Take a look on the Pinetribe website to find a laughter club close to you. Go to www.pinetribe.com/thomas-flindt/laughter-club

The reason Doctor Kataria called it Laughter Yoga was because, as a practitioner of yoga, he decided to incorporate elements of yogic breathing (*pranayama*) into the laughter exercises, in order to make them more effective. The word *yoga* comes from a Sanskrit word meaning 'union' or 'joining' because the aim of yoga is the union with the divine or with the self.

The anthropology of group laughter

A couple of years after I started working with laughter, I was contacted by a group of anthropology students from the Faculty of Social Sciences at Copenhagen University. The students, Janne, Mette, Henrik, Lea and Dominique, wanted to examine how participation in a laughter club affected people and what personal meaning it held for them. They wanted to examine the ways participation in a laughter club influenced people's daily lives and the nature of relationships within the club (both among participants and between the participants and their instructor).

This report[11], which makes for exciting reading, is about the extent to which participation in laughter clubs could be seen as ritual behaviour. The group told me that they intended to visit several different clubs as a part of their study and that they would participate as equals in the group laughter sessions they attended, reserving the right to be able to ask questions both before and after the sessions. The group's aim was to analyse the ritual aspects of group laughter through the lens of several different theoretical perspectives.

The findings
According to their report, group laughter does amount to a ritual, that is, something which is practiced in isolation from the routines of everyday life and demonstrates, through the use of special and specific activities, confirmation of one's own position within a cultural context.

They established that the instructor's role is vital in the creation, execution and maintenance of the ritual. They also reported that a ritual also implies the presence of collective action and so, apart from a group leader, there needs to be other participants involved if laughter in these clubs and gatherings is to be considered a form of ritual behaviour. These criteria are fulfilled in laughter clubs.

The ritual of laughter is, like other rituals, based on a principle of repetition. This means that both the instructor and participants are involved in creating, executing and maintaining the ritual in a formal pattern of set actions. Another argument that supports their thesis that laughter in this form can be interpreted as a ritual is that the instructor has complete monopoly on the use of speech during the ritual. Speech is strictly banned during group laughter, except for the instructor. When it is not possible to use words, this has the effect of cutting participants off from being able to pose questions.

I was really interested to learn this perspective as I have never thought of group laughter in this way before. I think about group laughter as providing a vehicle to the moment and as genuinely spontaneous. Happy hour, so to speak. It's also a place where you can come and develop your laughter; a form of therapy, which will help you to loosen up both physically and mentally; a short cut, a new road, straight to your laughter.

As you train yourself to let go of control during group laughter sessions, you will also become better at releasing control in everyday life. Stress and tension wear out the body like nothing else can. If you learn to release control, you will simultaneously find yourself becoming better at letting go of tension and stress. When we practise group laughter, we may also find ourselves acting out certain aspects of our lives or personalities which we normally repress.

In group laughter we are trying to create the conditions for a richer physical experience of the body. We are working to access our laughter on a deeper level. Humour and words come from an individual level of intellectual activity. When we talk to each other, we are also interpreting, evaluating and reflecting – we are "in our heads" and relating to each other from a mental level. In group laughter, you only need concern yourself with the laughter around you. In my opinion, this provides the best conditions to access laughter's marvellous universe.

In any case, I would always encourage laughter club participants to ask masses of questions, both before and after a laughter session, which is what normally happens anyway. If you ever feel negatively affected by or uncomfortable during a laughter session, then, of course, you should communicate this immediately – don't wait until the end of the session. Your laughter club is meant to be a safe place for you and the other participants, and it's your laughter leader's responsibility to make sure it is.

A human and anthropological triumph

One of the most interesting aspects of this report is the description of how the five anthropology students were personally influenced by their participation in laughter groups. Here is an extract taken directly from the report, describing their experiences:

> "Our most substantial and important method in this study has been that of participant observation. Via this method, we have personally experienced the ritual in practice and felt its effect on both body and mind. Our experience of the form of the ritual has led us to a better understanding of its content. Our expectations as to the effect of the

laughter ritual did not correspond with the experiences we actually had. We hadn't expected that the ritual would influence us, but we have to acknowledge both physical and mental effects. Bodily, it felt as though one had taken part in physical activity far more demanding than indicated by the laughter ritual itself. Whether we want to or not, we also have to acknowledge that the ritual also influenced our minds. It is hard to describe in words, but what we all felt afterwards was a greater readiness to smile and laugh, and we had attained a much more positive attitude towards everyday tasks and duties – those that are necessary, but which one doesn't always feel like doing."

World Laughter Day

This is a day of laughter shared across the world; a day when people laugh in New York, Sydney, Hamburg, and of course, in Copenhagen. It is a day when we celebrate laughter and the social ties that laughter creates between people. Madan Kataria held the first World Laughter Day in a square in Bombay on January 11th, 1999. 12,000 people turned up that day, on a race track just outside the city, to laugh together and to show their appreciation. The wonderful pictures of people laughing were sent around the world, bringing happiness and inspiring some very creative people to carry the torch of laughter forward.

A Danish advertising man, Jan Thygesen Poulsen, saw the pictures in Berlingske Tidende in January, 1999 and decided that he would bring this initiative to Denmark. Thus, on January 9th, 2000, Jan arranged the first celebration of World Laughter Day to be held in Denmark. Despite the cold weather, almost 10,000 Danes turned up on Copenhagen's town hall square, Rådhuspladsen, to laugh together that day.

Doctor Kataria had never dreamed that the World Laughter Day would spread so quickly and reach such cold and distant corners of the earth, so when he stepped onto Danish soil for the first time, to hold a workshop in the year 2000, he immediately changed the date of World Laughter Day. Laughter is now celebrated the world over on the first Sunday in May.

For several years now I have hosted World Laughter Day in Denmark, which takes place at Bakken fairground, north of Copenhagen, and each time has been a high point in my life!

CHAPTER #3

3

Group laughter in your living room

Try a one hour group laughter session and experience a great change in your life. Gather a group of friends together who would like to try something a little out of the ordinary. Of course, it's best if you can invite a skilled laughter coach to facilitate the session, but if you are a good communicator, then you will easily be able to do this on your own.

If you're facilitating it yourself, first tell your friends about the concept and ask if they would like to play (in essence, this is all really about play). Set aside an hour and agree that for that hour there will be nothing else on the agenda except laughter. Switch off the music, your mobile phones and anything else that might distract you mentally or physically. Make it clear to the group that you will be leading the session otherwise things can get a bit confusing. There are literally thousands of laughter exercises in existence and only your imagination can set the limit. If you happen to be the creative type, you can even make up your own exercises. I have included some of my very favourite ones in this chapter and at the end of this book.

Before you start, have the group silently reflect for a few moments on laughter. Explain to them that we have to access the body fully to be able to open up from within and let the laughter flow. In laughter sessions, we don't use jokes or humour to get us laughing. In fact, we don't even use words. Tell the group that they should not speak during the exercises, as only the group leader is permitted to talk.

When we speak, we begin to analyse. Laughter yoga is all about being fully in the body. Your truest, deepest and most authentic level of laughter comes from the stomach region. It is there we need to be. If the group members feel like talking to each other they should do so via non-verbal means. In other words, they should only use their bodies to communicate with each other.

Obviously, it is totally acceptable to act foolishly and crazily both before and during the exercise. Laughter should not be resisted, only the use of words!

First the group needs to learn a clapping ritual. Between each laughter exercise, clap to a common rhythm with added sounds. Clap "ho, ho" to the left and then "ha, ha, ha" to the right. Sway your body from side to side at the same time you clap and say "ho, ho - ha, ha, ha". Moving the body in this way helps to create a playful atmosphere. The clapping ritual is also a way for the leader to steer the group. Following each laughter exercise the leader starts this chanting and clapping "ho, ho – ha, ha, ha" and the rest of the group should follow along.

Laughter exercise 1: Quiet laughter with open mouth

Stand with your legs apart and put your hands on your stomach so you can feel its movement as you carry out this exercise. Let your head roll backwards and laugh very quietly. Open your mouth completely and let out the slightest of sounds - the kind of intensity you would use when breathing on a window pane. Keep this up for about 30-40 seconds.

Clap "Ho, ho – ha, ha, ha" etc

Breathing exercise

It is a good idea to breathe deeply together as a group between some of the following exercises. Place your awareness on your breath and centre yourself in the present moment. This will ensure that enough oxygen reaches the cells of your body. A great many people breathe from the chest upwards. This shallow breathing is also a symptom of stressed behaviour. Bend forwards, so that your hands and fingertips point towards the floor, just in front of your feet. Breathe in deeply through your nose whilst you raise yourself up and lift your hands above your head. Hold your breath for 5 seconds and then exhale slowly through your mouth.

Repeat this three times.

Laughter exercise 2: Hhhmmm laughter

The whole group should then stand in a circle again. For this exercise, the idea is to laugh with your mouth closed using a "hhhmmm" sound. Now is the time to establish eye contact with other group members when laughing. Eye contact allows a humorous spark to ignite and manifests genuine laughter. Look around the group while humming your laugh, "hhhmmm", with closed lips. Keep going for about 40-60 seconds.

Clap "Ho, ho – ha, ha, ha" etc

Stretching exercise

Lift your arms above your head and pretend you are picking apples from a very high tree. This exercise enables us to thoroughly stretch the solar plexus region. The solar plexus is fully activated when we laugh. Stretching between exercises in this way helps us to avoid injuries.

Laughter exercise 3: Greeting laughter

After warming up with the previous two exercises, we can now increase the tempo somewhat. Walk around and say hello to each other. In group laughter, we don't use words or each other's names to greet each other, but our laughter. If you can't remember how your laughter usually sounds, then just simulate something that approximates it.

Mingle with each other, make eye contact, shake each other by the hand and introduce yourself using your laugh.

Clap "Ho, ho – ha, ha, ha" etc

Repeat.

Breathing exercise

Bend forwards again, so that your hands and fingertips point towards the floor, just in front of your feet. Breathe in deeply through your nose, whilst you raise yourself up and lift your hands above your head. Hold your breath for 5 seconds and then exhale slowly through your mouth.

Repeat this three times.

Laughter exercise 4:
Ego laughter – laugh at yourself!

This exercise usually causes a great deal of hilarity. It provides a wonderful opportunity to laugh at ourselves. We hide a great deal of our laughter under our need to take ourselves seriously. If we can learn to laugh at ourselves then we give ourselves the chance to laugh much more frequently. In this exercise, you simply point your finger towards yourself, at your own chest or temple, and simply laugh.

Mingle amongst the other members of the group again, but remember, it is important to laugh at yourself. Point only at yourself as you wander around laughing.

Clap "Ho, ho – ha, ha, ha" etc

Face massage

Open your mouth slightly and lightly massage your jaw and other facial muscles with your fingertips for about 30-40 seconds. The muscles of your face can become rather sore when you laugh this much.

Laughter exercise 5:
Scolding laughter

When we laugh, we also let go of our tension and anger. The following exercise is a fun and effective way of releasing pent-up frustration and anger. The idea is to walk around, telling each other off with laughter.

Meet up with someone, stand face-to-face, lift your finger and just give that person a good dressing down – but only by using laughter.

You can start by looking angry as you do this, but slowly let your face become softer and more loving. Go around the group until you have told everybody off.

Clap "Ho, ho – ha, ha, ha" etc

Stretching exercise

Lift your arms and once again go through the motion of picking apples from a very tall tree in order to stretch your solar plexus.

Laughter exercise 6: Whispering laughter

Laughter doesn't always have to be loud. Walk around again, put your hand to your mouth, and quietly whisper your laughter into each other's ear. This exercise usually causes a lot of sniggering and funny faces. Most people find out how difficult it is to keep laughter quiet.

Clap "Ho, ho – ha, ha, ha" etc

Laughter exercise 7: One-metre laughter

An Indian tailor invented this exercise. Here you measure a 'metre of laughter' with your arm. Lift your left arm and stretch it out to the side. Put your right hand on your left arm as if you were going to measure its length, like a tailor would when measuring cloth. Move your hand to the elbow as you make the following sound: "aeaeaeaeaeae". Then, move your hand up to your left shoulder and repeat this sound.

Move your hand on again to the opposite shoulder and repeat "aeaeae-aeaeae". Open the right arm out fully now and laugh, "ha ha ha ha ha". This exercise is really fun and usually causes a great deal of hilarity.

Clap "Ho, ho – ha, ha, ha" etc

Breathing exercise

As before, bend forwards, breathe in deeply through your nose, then raise yourself up and lift your hands above your head. Hold your breath for 5 seconds and then exhale slowly through your mouth.

Repeat this three times.

Laughter exercise 8: Friendship laughter-colleague laughter

This exercise combines the acceptance that naturally lies in laughter with a practical example. In the exercise you work in pairs. Stand face-to-face, tilt your head a little to one side and then pat each other lightly on the shoulder as you laugh quietly and kindly with each other. Go around the room meeting new partners, patting each other on the shoulder and laughing in this friendly way. If you are in the company of people you know well, then you can even give each other a laughing hug.

Clap "Ho, ho – ha, ha, ha" etc

Face massage

Open your mouth slightly and lightly massage your jaw and other face muscles with your fingertips for about 30-40 seconds.

Free laughter

These were the introductory exercises. Now the group should move into free laughter. Sit together on the floor, preferably in a way where everyone can make eye contact with each other. It is important that everyone sits at the same level. However, if anyone present is unable to sit comfortably on the floor, then obviously they should be invited to use a chair or whatever works best for them. (You could put everyone on chairs so you are all at the same level and they don't feel left out).

No intentional exercises are involved in this part of the session. Just allow the laughter to flow freely as everyone maintains eye contact. If the laughter doesn't seem to be manifesting, then fake it until you make it! If you can't get the laughter started, then cheat a bit – pretend to laugh at first and you will find that suddenly this will shift into genuine laughter. A fake laugh is just as infectious as a real laugh – it's also been found in research that people are not good at distinguishing between fake and real smiles. It is thought that this is because it is better for helping people get along if they do not always know what each other is feeling[12]! Look at the person sitting beside you and send them a laugh.

Note: it's important to accept the fact that people do not laugh for the same amount of time – nobody should feel self-conscious about their laughter being different from someone else's. Tell the group that it is OK to have a little pause now and then, to relax and enjoy the good energy that is present in the room, but emphasise that it is important that nobody starts to talk. Allocate about 15-20 minutes for free laughter and see what happens.

Silent meditation

When the leader of the group can feel that the laughter is fading, then it is time to close the session. Finish off with a silent meditation. The body has been extremely active for the past 20-40 minutes, so a state of total relaxation should now be encouraged. Ask everyone to sit or lie quietly with closed eyes for about 5-10 minutes and to notice the changes that laughter has created in their bodies. Slowly, bring everyone 'back' again and invite them to look around at each other and notice what the laughter has created. It might be enlightening to go round the group and listen to each other's experiences of the group laughter session.

Warning!
The following health risks are associated with laughter yoga:

- Too much laughter can actually worsen symptoms of severe colds and flu.

- If you are pregnant, then you should be careful about laughing too much. Violent laughter can actually induce labour.

- Laughter yoga could be problematic if you suffer from incontinence as our muscles relax when we laugh.

CHAPTER #4

4.1
Why we laugh:
To free our laughing self

A smile is a window to your soul – laughter is the door.
- Neale Donald Walsch

To dare to be your authentic self is to be truly free. Yet if you wish to experience this freedom, you have to be willing to let go of the opinions other people have about you. You also have to become liberated from the limiting and critical thoughts you have about yourself.

You have to allow yourself the freedom to be the person you are and this means being able to express yourself without judging yourself.

If you look down on and criticise others, undoubtedly you also look down on and criticise yourself. Like many other Danes, I have been chained to what is called *Jante's Law*, a powerful Danish norm, an unwritten 'rule', which encourages a social climate of mediocrity. It is a mechanism of social control, which works by preventing people from believing that they might in any way be special or extraordinary.

The Danes like to make fun of *Jante's Law*, but the truth is that many of them actually live by it.

I realised some time ago, that the judgments I had about others were also judgments I had about myself. I found that when I couldn't allow others their own 'personal style' or accept that they expressed themselves in a certain way it was because I couldn't really allow my own personal style or expression to manifest.

The laughter club

On February 20th, 2003, I attended a laughter club for the very first time in my life. I had no idea what I was letting myself in for, but I was enormously excited. I walked through the door of Østerbro Laughter Club - the first of its kind in Denmark - on my own. As I walked around, introducing myself to those who had already arrived, I noted how I immediately started judging several people in the room. There were many different types of people gathered there that evening. Some looked completely ordinary, others were more hippy-like, wearing scruffy clothes.

That February evening I discovered new sides to myself. The intimacy and empathy that arose from the laughter in that group was an unbelievable experience for me. I was surprised and overwhelmed that laughter could be initiated without using humour. The bond that was established there through laughter was extraordinary. At 7 p.m. everyone in the group was a stranger to me. By 8.30 p.m., I felt closely connected to everyone present. All the judgments I had made when I first walked through the door had now disappeared and I felt that the people I had laughed with that evening were some of the most fantastic people I had ever met in my life. Over the following days, I couldn't understand why everyone was smiling at me. Then I looked in the mirror and discovered that the look in my eyes had become warmer and brighter. My face had changed its expression. My whole being had changed its expression.

The shadow side

We learn about ourselves through our contact with others. A couple of years ago, I read an article about 'the shadow side'[13]. The theme was that we humans contain every manner of expression and feeling. Everything. We express a great deal of these through our personality, and those we cannot express are still there inside us anyway. They lie in the shadow side of our being and are not consciously embraced.

Maybe there is a particular feeling or a certain behaviour that you are not able to show the world. Maybe you don't want to or maybe you have been raised not to reveal certain emotions or states. For example, if you are female, you might have been raised to be a quiet girl. You were taught that you mustn't speak loudly, and that you mustn't be outspoken. This might mean that when you see a woman like (for example) Roseanne Barr or Ruby Wax, you feel very uncomfortable. According to what you have been taught to believe, behaving like this is wrong. You find it hard to accept such behaviour in other people *precisely because you cannot express this aspect of yourself*. Feeling provoked by someone else in this way can help you to become more conscious of suppressed or blocked aspects of yourself, because you are directly confronted with them through the other person's behaviour.

In the future, when you find yourself provoked by someone because of their personality or behaviour, you now have a choice: you can choose to be provoked, or you can reflect on whether this person is actually behaving in a way you, in reality, would like to be able to behave yourself.

Exercise: Embrace other people's 'funny little ways'

When something about another person annoys you, embrace that character trait and try to think of it as a charming foible.

Think to yourself that it is one of the things that makes that person special and unique.

Ask yourself - does it annoy you because it is something that annoys you about yourself? Or maybe because it's something that you wish you were able to do yourself?

Next time someone in your life (friend, colleague, partner, child or anyone!) annoys you, make a list of their funny little ways and try to find ways to celebrate them.

Focusing on allowing others to be their authentic selves opens the door for you to be your authentic, laughing, self. If you can learn to cherish other people's 'funny little ways', you will eventually learn to cherish your own.

Your laughing self

Humour is individual - laughter is universal

- Thomas Flindt

Children express feelings, opinions and experiences much more freely than we adults do. The more you are able to be your true self, the more often you will celebrate life and yourself through laughter. When you can really feel your body, then the energy and joy of life is there inside you like a feather, constantly tickling your insides. Bubbles of happiness lie just under the surface of your skin, you are released, you are free, you don't ask questions about your laughter – you just laugh.

The advantage of working with the laughter of our inner child is that it is common to everyone. We were born with it and we still contain this childlike glee within us – this is our laughing self that we lose touch with as we grow older. Laughter lies inherent within us from the day of our birth and we are able to express it from a very young age.

When we adults observe a month-old baby lying on its back, chuckling away, we don't think, "Great sense of humour that baby has" - we just enjoy watching it express its happiness and seeing how freely it can laugh. Babies and children don't need a reason to laugh – they just laugh. For the first many years of our lives, we laugh from our bellies and our bodies, and not from our brain. For the first years of our lives, we laugh to express our spontaneous joy and to release the rush of warmth that is happiness, which surges through our body in the present, lived moment.

Many of us adults hold the conviction that we need to have a good reason to laugh. If we are in the company of someone who suddenly bursts out laughing, we will want to know what they are laughing about. And we want to know right now. We don't think, "How lovely that they can laugh like that!" We don't begin to laugh simply because we hear such delightful laughter. No, we have to have a good reason for laughing along with them. And we need a good reason because most adult laughter comes from the mind and not from the heart or the body.

Children don't ask questions when they hear a spontaneous, hearty chuckle. They just laugh too. Children allow the energy of laughter to just stream through them. Laughter comes so easily to a child. It is second nature to them and demands no explanations. It's natural!

The adult brain wants the whys and the wherefores, the background and the context: "Why are you laughing?" it asks. This constant impulse to explain the world places restrictions and limits on pure, unadulterated experience. So it is easier to just not laugh because then we won't be called to account for ourselves. If we want to create more freedom and space for ourselves, then it's a really good idea to start by giving others this privilege.

Try and enjoy the spontaneous laughter of others. Smile at them supportively or just laugh along with them. Enjoy the blast of good energy that their laughter brings. Don't race into your head, demanding explanations. Stay in the moment, feel the joy and let yourself be infected by it.

In order to open up to your laughter at a deeper level and get back to your laughing self, it is important to understand the laughter that belongs to your inner child. The goal is to be conscious and allow yourself to laugh like a child, as well as an adult.

Therefore, we need to address the issue of humour versus laughter. Many of us assume that these two things are the same. It is true that they make a good combination and that they influence each other, but they are actually two completely different things. Humour is an individual characteristic and takes many different forms according to the character and preferences of each person. Laughter is universal and stems from the body in the same way for everybody. If you laugh heartily with someone that doesn't speak the same language as you, they will be perfectly clear about what is going on. More than likely, they will laugh with you or smile back.

On the other hand, if you try and tell someone from a different country a popular joke, they probably won't have the slightest idea what you are talking about. Humour is culturally and individually determined. Laughter is universal and common to us all.

When you learn to laugh unconditionally, it frees you from yourself and from the opinions of others. Laughter becomes a stream of natural life energy, which flows through you more and more often in your daily life. You experience unconditional joy when you can truly laugh without having a reason. This is the path to your laughing self.

Exercise in unconditional laughter

Next time you see or hear a grown woman or man break out into laughter, just laugh along with them, *even if you haven't got a clue what they are laughing about*. You can always ask later, "What were we actually laughing about?" – and then you'll have the chance to laugh all over again.

When you become really good at laughing without a reason, you will also find yourself understanding and respecting your body better. You will be able to give yourself more easily to the feelings which arise in your body. When you get good at laughing *without* a reason, you also become better at laughing *for* a reason. You will simply find that your laughter has gained a greater range of nuance and that it resonates through your body for longer.

In children, laughter is a language in itself. This is the case for adults too, but sadly, many of us have simply forgotten the language. I wonder if you can remember the last time you really gave in to an uncontrolled belly laugh? A rolling-round-on-the floor, splitting-your-sides, kind of laughter - a fit of laughter that just went on and on and on – time and space dissolved and all that remained was pure and unadulterated laughter.

Do you remember? I am certain that if you can recall such an experience, you will remember that you were not alone. You were with the person that made it possible. You are probably thinking now that this laughing fit arose because you shared the same sense of humour. This is probably true, but you had something else. You had the same frequency of laughter, and you had the courage to throw yourselves overboard for a moment.

When the shrieking and roaring just carries on and on, it is because the laughter has become a language. Your laughter is simply understood by the other person you are laughing with. It is like looking in a mirror, or hitting a ball against a wall. You send out your laughter and the person you are with sends it back again. The point is to understand your laughter, appreciate your laughter and give it space to exist. The laughter is enough in itself. It is a language in itself and it is not dependent on humour.

Humour and laughter contain unlimited possibilities. Most people know the formula: *Humour releases laughter*. True, and boy, has humour released a great deal of laughter throughout history! Thank you, humour! But here is a new formula: *Laughter releases humour*. It works both ways! They are like two friends who walk hand in hand through life – through *your* life. A well-developed sense of humour leads to some good experiences of laughter.

A well-developed laughter likewise leads to a good sense of humour. In the practice of group laughter and in laughter clubs, we have created a forum for laughing without reason. We have created a place, a free space, where we don't need to explain why we are laughing. We perform specific laughter exercises and intentionally use the body to open up to the state of laughter. And we don't rely on humour to do this.

However, what I have noticed, as have many others who have participated in group laughter, is that such practices actually create humour. Once we actually have got going and have laughed for some time, we suddenly begin to notice all the funny things around us.

We find a wealth of new reasons to laugh and our humour and laughter becomes filled with variety and nuance. When you have tried laughing like this a couple of times, you will get to know the language of laughter better. You might find that just a simple, funny noise or an inspiring laugh will be enough to ignite the flame of your laughing self.

The most important thing is to let yourself be infected by the laughter of others, without having to know what they are laughing about. The point of departure in group laughter is to laugh for no reason; to just relax and be immersed in laughter itself. You listen out for the funny, the lovely, and the infectious in each other's laughter.

Then you take this out into 'real life' and when you hear someone laughing heartily, you respond by setting your own laughter loose.

Lis and the beavers - my first and greatest public fit of laughter

On June 18th, 2003, I went to a birthday party in the grounds of the Tivoli amusement park in Copenhagen. My friend Lis Nielsen – one of the most fantastic people I know – was turning 60 that day. Lis had invited her closest family and friends out to eat. It was a beautiful day. The sun was shining and everyone was happy as we dined in the old gardens. After the meal, the plan was to enjoy some of the fairground rides. We came to "The Mine", which in the old days was known as "The Tubs", where you ride in tub-like boats through a system of water channels in a grotto or mine, which is manned by a bunch of hard-working clockwork beavers.

I had the great privilege of sitting next to the birthday girl on this ride. One of the reasons I admire Lis so much is that she has so wonderfully kept the child in her alive. She can still play and meet the world as if she were five years old.

So there we were, sailing around the grotto past all these model beavers. Lis began to wave at the beavers as we sailed by, calling to them "Hi there". With a cute face and a sugar-sweet voice, she greeted the many beavers as we passed by with a "Hi there, honey". The situation was comic, crazy, fun and fantastic all at the same time.

I began to giggle and when Lis looked at me, she too began to laugh. After giggling together for a while, I began to feel a much larger wave of laughter rising within me. In fact, it felt as if a gigantic laughing fit was about to erupt out of my body and I just knew that I was going to allow it to flow. I knew I was going to let myself laugh just as much as I wanted. The laughing fit that broke there, in the dark mine, had an overwhelming effect on myself and everyone else in the grotto. The other birthday guests, in the boats in front of us, were soon laughing along with us. They didn't know what we were laughing about, but our laughter was so hearty and resounding, that they couldn't help but be influenced by it.

The boats behind us were full of people we didn't know, but it didn't take long before they too had been infected by the laughter. Everyone roared with laughter the entire way around the mine and even when we finally reach 'land' at the end of the ride, we were all still laughing wildly. In fact, every single boat came to the end of the ride full of laughing people – all sparked off by me simply allowing myself to laugh uninhibitedly. After this experience, I knew that something fundamental had changed in me. I could permit myself to have a laughing fit in public. I felt that I was now truly capable of enjoying life and of directly and spontaneously letting my laughing self be free. My work and my laughter practice were beginning to have a significant effect on my self-expression.

The Aha! experience

I just love when I experience a radical shift in my understanding. When something I thought I knew everything about suddenly shows itself to be quite different, or to contain a dimension that I had not previously discovered. We usually hold quite tightly to our convictions. There is nothing really wrong with that. But, sometimes we hold on so tightly that we are not open to anything new. Through our deeply held beliefs and opinions, many of us maintain our worlds in particular set forms. Sometimes, we forget that the world is in a constant state of change and development. And it is not just the world that is constantly developing; every individual on this planet is also constantly moving forwards.

When you are open to the new, the new is also open to you. I can't guarantee a success rate of 100% on the basis of this statement, but it is certainly worth a try.

New humour – new friends

I have a good friend called Marcus. However, I had never imagined that Marcus and I would become such good friends. For several years, our paths often crossed because we had friends in common. Yet, I never felt the urge to get to know him any better - I just didn't consider him as a potential friend. In fact, if the truth be told, for several years, I had assigned Marcus to the category of 'dull people', with no hope of salvation.

I had put the 'boring' label on Marcus and placed him on a shelf with other boring things.

And then one Saturday evening, something happened. I was in a particularly good mood and allowed myself to laugh at one of Marcus' comments. It wasn't because Marcus said anything particularly funny, it was just the rather dry way he said it that was amusing.

Of course, the situation was a bit special, because it happened precisely on a day when I had a little more energy and resources for someone like Marcus and was therefore more open to him. As I was laughing, I noticed that I had opened up and let Marcus in. I had opened up for the person Marcus and for his unique 'Marcus-Humour'. It was a total 'Aha! experience' – a completely new brand of humour to laugh at. It was a gift!

Today, Marcus and I have a great friendship and I thoroughly enjoy his company, in which I enter into a whole new universe of humour. It is as though an underdeveloped side of me is being slowly pushed out into the light.

Just think, if I had started laughing with Marcus years before... what a gift that would have been!

Exercises in opening up

The next time you meet someone new, imagine that they are your best friend, and show them the kind of acceptance and openness that you would show to someone you know and love. You might be surprised by the connections you can make!

The next time you encounter a sense of humour you don't find funny, make a special effort to laugh. Show them the kind of attention you would show to someone you think is the funniest person in the world. Like I was surprised by Marcus' unique brand of humour, you might experience the pleasure of enjoying something completely unexpected. When you are open to new people, you are open to new sides in yourself. When you are open to new kinds of humour, you are open to developing your own sense of humour.

As adults we observe children and often think, "How easy it is to be a child!" But we should ask ourselves occasionally: "What actually makes it so difficult to be an adult?"

The truth is that it's also adult responsibilities, and not just adult attitudes, that make it difficult to be an adult, but we can still learn from children's contact with their authentic laughing self, and learn to carry our burdens more lightly by not limiting our selves unnecessarily, and staying in touch with the source of laughter inside us.

There are some things we do and know instinctively as children, that we forget as adults. We can bring them back into our lives and get back in touch with our laughing self.

Anger and sadness - the brothers and sisters of your laughing self:

Anger

It is important to release your anger. Anger can smother your happiness like a heavy blanket. If you have unreleased anger within you, then you probably don't feel happy that often. Anger causes tension throughout our entire body. This inner tension is unhealthy and puts great strain on our internal organs. Release your anger, even if you have to shout and scream it out. Talking things out doesn't always work with anger. Shouting and screaming can be very healthy and very relieving. However, in contrast to a whoop of enthusiasm, you should consider carefully where you let out your scream of pent up rage.

Perhaps it isn't the person triggering your anger right now who is the real reason for your anger. Anger can build up slowly over a long period and although it finally has to come out, try and find out where it really comes from and whether the person currently on the receiving end really deserves this treatment. As with laughter and tears, many people have a hard time accepting anger as a part of their natural repertoire of expression. If, when you see other people expressing their anger, you find it grossly inappropriate you might be the kind of person who has repressed their own angry feelings.

But the sensation of anger bubbling up is the chance for a feeling, an energetic impulse, a story, an experience to be released. When anger makes itself known, you mustn't overrule it, because if you allow yourself to let go of your anger, you have the chance to release the experience or story attached to it which you no longer wish to be a part of. If you don't work with it, anger will remain in your subconscious, retaining the power to drag you back into the past. When we release anger, we let go of feelings we don't want to have pent up in our body any longer and can return to the present moment and enjoy life.

If you find it very challenging to deal with your feelings of anger then find a good therapist who can help you find ways to constructively work with the process. In my mind, there is no doubt that anger is the worst enemy of happiness.

All your physical and emotional expressions are a part of your personality. The more you allow your body and your feelings free passage, the more you will come across as the person you really are. The joy of life is about being present, experiencing your feelings honestly and being able to express the happiness you experience in this moment. The joy of life is also about being able to express sorrow, anger and bitterness, if these are the feelings which are occupying you right now. If your body and mind are filled with anger and bitterness, then there isn't much of a chance that a space for happiness will be created. If you feel angry, it must be expressed and released, in just the same way as when you feel happy.

Elise – the woman who could not laugh

Over the years, I have laughed with many thousands of people. One particular person who made a great impression on me, was a woman called Elise. Elise contacted me because she wanted to visit the laughter club I had set up. This was, however, a rather special situation - Elise was unable to laugh. Elise was 39 years old and said she could not remember the last time she had laughed. I was very touched by Elise's story and said that, of course, she was welcome to come to the laughter club any time she wanted. Elise knew she wouldn't be able to laugh during the sessions but she just wanted to be in a room together with people who were laughing.

Laughter is a very strong expression of solidarity and a powerful connection is created when we laugh together as a group. To see Elise just sitting there silently, while the others howled and screeched around her was one of the most moving things I have ever experienced. It requires great courage to dare to sit in a group like that without being able to participate on equal terms. However, Elise was very determined that something needed to change in her life. She turned up to every single session without fail, sitting there quietly while the others let rip. The energy in our laughter sessions is enormous. The vibrations of happiness are very high.

Likewise, it is very motivating to hear and see other people laughing, to see them daring to let go of control. I am sure that this is the motivation and inspiration Elise needed. After about six months, Elise started to laugh authentically and was able to sustain her laughter during our sessions. Today, Elise is one of the most loyal members of the club.

Sadness

We often measure our happiness by how much we laugh and smile in our daily life. Of course, there is a connection between laughing, smiling and being happy. Smiling and laughing are a method to transform and express your energy, but they are not the reason for your happiness. Your happiness is a feeling or a state - laughing and smiling can be a way to get you there, but you don't need to smile or laugh to be happy.

If you have just lost a job, if you are recovering from the end of a relationship, or maybe if life has not turned out the way you planned or hoped for, you might find it hard to laugh and smile today. This is why I want you to take a good look at the brothers and sisters of laughter. The brother and sisters of laughter are crying and anger. Laughing is all about transforming your energy and getting you back into balance. Crying or expressing anger is also about transforming your energy and getting you back into balance. Sometimes we're afraid to let go of anger and tears. It might be too intense for us to cry or to be angry, but it is often the only way to let go of old feelings that got stuck in our system.

If you find it hard to cry or if you find it hard to be angry, you might find it hard to laugh too. Sometimes people need to cry or to be angry before they can laugh again. Those emotions that are connected to tears and anger will live on top of your laughter and wait for you to release them first. It is that simple. But it is not a simple practice.

This practice is about being honest with yourself and doing what you have to do to get back into balance. If you have lost a job, if you are recovering from the end of a relationship, or if your life did not turn out the way you planned, it is time to make a new plan and a new story to believe in – but before you make a new plan and before you write a new story, you need to release your old story.

Exercise: Letting go

Spend time writing down your old story. Write down all the things you used to dream and hope for - write everything you know and need to express about this dream you once had. Make sure you keep writing until you've described your dream fully. When you are sure you have written everything that is on your mind and in your system, you need to read this story to yourself. Read it with great passion.

If sadness or anger is in your system you need to cry with great passion and you need to be angry with great passion as you read this story of yours. Accept that this was once your dream and accept that you need to let it go now. Maybe you don't need to let everything in this dream go, but you need to let this version of this dream go. Cry or be angry with no limits until it is done. It's done when you start laughing again.

Laughing is all about accepting this moment. When the old story has left your system - you will start to laugh again.

CHAPTER #4

4.2
Why we laugh: To communicate and connect with others

The body communicates through laughter

Laughter is one of the ways in which your body communicates with the world. According to behavioural psychologists, 55% of all our communication is expressed via the body (i.e. through non-verbal communication). In his book *Silent Messages*, Professor Albert Mehrabian concludes that words make up a much smaller percentage of our overall communication – around 7%, with tone of voice being responsible for the last 38%.

Your first attempts at communication

As a baby, you had two major channels of expression: laughter and tears. Thus, at the start of life, laughter is a very pure form of communication.

The first time you communicated was before your speech and language capacities had developed, before your humour and intellect had developed. You were just a few hours old when you felt the first impulse to express your opinion about life through crying. When you were just a few weeks old, the first smile appeared on your lips. After a few more, your zest for life had grown even further and you began to chuckle.

When you were a couple of months old, you really began to fully respond to your life experiences as the first laughter rolled through your body. You wanted to tell your parents that you thought the world was fantastic and that you were really very satisfied with your lot.

For the first many years of our lives, laughter is a spontaneous expression of joy – a pure form of communication. That part of laughter is important to remember and hold on to. Your first original laughter was a natural, authentic and unconditional event. Do you remember what it was like to laugh like that?

We laugh to connect and form bonds with each other

Laughter is a signal of acceptance and acknowledgement. When we laugh with others, we demonstrate that we are open to them and that we receive them. With our laughter and smiles, we show that we care about them. We usually laugh spontaneously, yet at other times, we bring forth laughter in a more artificial or intentional way. We communicate both unconsciously and consciously with our laughter. Perhaps you are familiar with the situation where your friend is trying hard to be funny, even though they don't have one ounce of wit in their entire body?

They make a brave attempt to tell you a joke and get you to laugh but they just haven't got the touch. They're a nice person and you want to show them that you accept and acknowledge them, and therefore, you laugh at their rather stale joke. Your friend is searching for the acceptance and recognition that lies in your laughter.

You probably have also experienced the situation where you and a group of friends are sitting telling jokes to each other, and even though you don't quite understand what one particular joke is really about, you want to signal that you are a part of the group and therefore you laugh along, despite not having really got the point of the joke.

There are many examples of such intentional laughter. This shows us that many of us use laughter as a conscious tool to communicate and forge connections. If you can be more accepting of yourself when you laugh like this, then I can guarantee that you will bring more laughter into your life. Determined or intentional laughter is perhaps not the most enjoyable form of laughter, but by acknowledging it as a legitimate part of your communicative repertoire you also acknowledge that it is a legitimate part of you.

Over the course of our lives, we find that the friends we make are the ones who have been with us through particularly good times (a lot of us make childhood or university friends who stay with us our whole lives). There is evidence that the hormone oxytocin is part of the bonding process 14, and is produced during positive social behaviour. As we know, laughter helps us produce a whole raft of good hormones, including oxytocin, so laughter can help us take a short cut to connection with one another, by producing the perfect environment for us to bond. We can use this brilliant shortcut to build a stronger sense of connectedness and closeness at work, at home and in our communities.

Supermarket laughter
The success with *Four Systems* led to several other companies approaching me about workplace laughter. *Super Best*, a supermarket in Allerød, were sure that it was something they could benefit from. In January 2005, I was contacted by the manager, Hernrik Kjærulf, who asked to meet me. The friendly grocer offered me a cup of coffee and I asked him why he was interested in a laughter course in the store.

Henrik Kjærulf replied, "Look Thomas, our store is just like any other store of its kind. The goods we sell are more or less the same as in any other supermarket. If we are to make any difference at all, then we have to do something special for our workers. I want to do something that is directly aimed at the welfare and wellbeing of my employees." This was definitely an attitude I could relate to. We agreed that, over the course of 14 days in April, each working day in the store would begin with laughter.

All the employees –around a hundred, both full-time and part-time – laughed loudly and heartily when I turned up unannounced at a staff meeting in March and told them about the Super Best laughter project arranged for April. For 14 working days, the entire staff of this orderly supermarket gathered at 9:10 a.m. sharp in front of the cash registers and laughed for 15 minutes every morning. The store opened its doors at 9:30 a.m., giving us time to wind down our laughter session in time to meet the customers.

The local newspaper, *Allerød Nyt*, sent a representative, hoping for a good story. The young journalist could barely hold the pen in his hand as he shook with laughter that Wednesday morning in April. The journalist could not resist giving in to the laughter and left taking notes and doing interviews until after the laughter had subsided. The journalist then approached a young sales assistant, Anne, and asked her how she felt about having started the last ten working days in this way.

Anne answered, "It has changed the atmosphere in the entire store. We are more connected with each other. Before, people just went around in their own worlds, just taking care of what was happening in their own departments. Now we say 'hi' to each other more often and we make witty remarks when we see each other across the store. The day passes more quickly when you are having fun at work – suddenly, it is time to go home". Neither was the manager in doubt that it had been a good initiative for the company: "I have achieved a much better relationship with my staff," concluded Henrik Kjærulf. "I am now on first name terms with my employees. Before they would call me 'Boss' or 'Mr Kjærulf' – now they call me 'Henrik'." Following on from those 14 days of laughter, *Super Best* continued to laugh every Monday or Friday morning for the next 6 months. In this period, the store's turnover rose by 8%. It was the biggest increase in profits that *Super Best* had experienced in 7 years.

Laughing with the people in your community will help you create a stronger, funnier and more peaceful community. When we laugh we let go of our fear and we open up to our best potential. There is a tendency in many communities to focus on fear and worry, and suspicion of one another – before long we end up just focusing on the bad situations that might happen and ways in which other people might be able to do us wrong. But how can we be at peace with each other and enjoy our lives together if we are constantly suspicious and afraid? It is so much more powerful to have faith in each other and to be open and loving to each other.

Expect the best from the people in your community and find opportunities to laugh with them – you could host a laughter session and invite your neighbours, or you could even organise a laughter festival

in your area! You'll be surprised of the ways you can connect when you open yourselves up to each other with laughter.

Laughter also reinforces bonds and connections that are already there. Laughing together strengthens existing relationships, smooths out tension and brings joy. You could try laughing together to reconnect with old friends, or to bring your family closer together.

Hellerup ladies' lodge
In November 2004, I was contacted by a ladies' lodge in Hellerup. The lodge was made up of 10-12 women, all with established careers. Apart from being members of the same lodge, these women were also friends socially. The women met once every second month for an event, which included a lecture or a workshop of some kind.

I had been booked that autumn night to provide a mini-laughter course for the group. I arrived at 9 p.m. and stepped into a beautiful and superbly furnished Hellerup villa. I walked into the large dining room and, seated around the oval dining table, were 12 lovely women, all looking very comfortable after their meal together.

The first part of my lecture was theoretical and concerned with how we use laughter in our lives. When it came to doing the group laughter exercises, we went into the neighbouring room, where there was floor space for everyone. We started by loosening up the body. The women threw themselves into the exercises with great enthusiasm. After around eight exercises we moved into free laughter, sitting together on the floor in a circle so everyone had eye contact with each other. It didn't take long for the free laughter to develop into an uncontrollable laughing fit for most of the assembled women.

When you know each other as well as these women did, it is even easier to open up to a deeper level of laughter. Things were going well. I had a good feeling that the women knew each other really well and therefore I decide to end the free laughter session lying down. To create even more vibration and even more energy, I arranged us all so that everyone was lying with their head on another person's belly. The result was a huge square made up of women lying with their heads on each other's stomachs. The free laughter continued. I could hear that some of the women's laughter had become even deeper and louder. Everyone, including me, lay on the floor dissolved in pure laughter.

You could *feel* the laughter as well as hear it. A full-on sensory experience. Suddenly, one of the women began screaming. Really screaming. Oh my god, I thought, things are getting really wild. One of the other women looked at me at asked if it was OK for them to scream. "Of course", I answered. So, they all began screaming wildly at the top of their lungs. There I was, lying on the floor, my head on the belly of one of these wonderful Hellerup women, surrounded by a chorus of wild shrieking. It was an experience that is difficult to describe in words. It was very, very powerful and really amazing!

Using smiles and laughter to build bridges

From my childhood growing up in the 70s and 80s, the Cold War was always a fear factor in my life. The Cold War was often in the news and for many years there was an intense fear of war in many peoples hearts in both Europe and the US. Things started to change in the late 80s with the fall of the Berlin Wall. But something amazing happened in the 90s.

I think many people felt the same way as me when they saw the American president Bill Clinton and the Russian president Boris Yeltsin having a laughing fit together. I really felt at peace when I saw this on TV in 1995. The Cold War had finally been thawed by laughter. See the video on www.pinetribe.com/thomas-flindt/cold-war

The merry criminal

Some years ago, there was a high-profile case of an insurance swindle here in Denmark. It was the biggest fraud case in Danish history and centred on two very well-known and charismatic personalities: Kurt Thorsen and Rasmus Trads. False signatures had been used to embezzle millions. Kurt Thorsen was the financial entrepreneur who had plans to build a whole chain of hotels in Spain. Rasmus Trads was the man with an insurance company behind him, who could provide the necessary security to assure funding for the project. However, Rasmus Trads was actually not authorised to offer security on the funding that Kurt Thorsen so desperately wanted, and the investment document drawn up was based on false signatures. The burning question at the centre of the court case was, *did Thorsen know that the Trads had forged his boss' signature?*

Like many other Danes at that time, I sat glued to the TV screen every evening, to watch these two men come down the steps of the high court each evening and make their comments to the press. On the right, in a blue suit, the five foot nothing Kurt Thorsen and on the left in a gray suit, Rasmus Trads, towering over him at six foot four. I must admit that I was a big fan of Kurt Thorsen (the finance man, who insisted that he didn't know about the false signatures), who with his little round head and his charming mannerisms had won my sympathies and convinced me of his innocence.

In retrospect, I can now see exactly why! Here is a man who, despite a long day in court behind him, a six to eight year prison sentence hanging over his head and the press crowding in on him, was able to laugh delightfully, as he proclaimed his innocence. With his smile and his laughter, he radiated relaxation and a surplus of personal resources. He gave the impression of being on top of things - and therefore of being able to take things easy. He had a genuine, hearty and relaxed laugh, without a trace of nervous laughter.

Seen through my TV eyes, he was an innocent man. It would be impossible to be so laid back, I thought to myself, if he really had something to hide.

Was Kurt Thorsen conscious of the communicative value of his laughter and smiling? Probably. It clearly had an effect on me. I think that Thorsen might have intentionally used his laughter to signal the calmness and clarity an innocent man would have. It turned out that the judge didn't feel like laughing along! Despite his fun and brightness, Thorsen was sentenced to six years imprisonment.

I still give him credit: the man is surely a master in non-verbal communication!

Laughter can wound

Laughter is a powerful force, and it can be used to hurt as well as heal. We only have to look at people like Rush Limbaugh or Bill Maher, who use humour to criticise and to hurt, and to encourage others to do the same, to know that laughter can be used to attack as well as to embrace others.

Children also use laughter to hurt each other, when they gang up to pick on another child. It could be glasses, nose, freckles or ears that single a child out to be jeered at. In these situations, laughter can really hurt. This is a side of laughter - scornful laughter - that we as adults, and of course as children, must be very aware of. If someone has experienced too much mocking laughter in their life, it can have some very negative associations. If someone has been bullied or abused using laughter, then they will understandably start getting anxious when others begin to laugh, afraid that they might be made the object of ridicule. This can be an obstacle to openly sharing in laughter, and to letting out our laughing self.

In public places, I have noticed that there are often those who look a little perturbed, even frightened, when others begin to laugh. These are probably the ones who have been hurt over the years by laughter. It is really important that we teach our children to laugh with and not against each other. It is also important that we dare to step in when laughter is used as a weapon against others.

Living a life where you associate laughter with bad experiences can't be a particularly enjoyable life. Therefore, be brave and step in when someone is abusive with laughter. Bullying and abuse are not uncommon problems amongst adults, but we can put a stop to it by stepping in when we see it happening by letting the perpetrators know that it is not acceptable to do this.

We communicate our love with laughter

We laugh more when we are in love. If you are in love right now, you will probably agree with me. If it's been some time since you were last in love, then try and think back to your teenage years, when you giggled at everything the object of your desire said, or you went to great lengths to try to make your special person laugh. We use laughter in this way to express our devotion to and acceptance of another person.

Of course, there is also another reason why we laugh more when we are in love. This is because we are much more present in the moment. You have finally met the one and only. The most perfect and most fantastic person, the very one you have been waiting for all this time, is standing there right in front of you.

When we are in love, everything else just pales into insignificance. A fire could start in the house next door, and World War III might break out, and it won't matter one little bit – because you are here, right now, with your true love.

New love pulls us into the moment. When we are very conscious and present in the moment, we can also feel the constant stream of life energy and happiness that flows through our bodies. Laughter is a natural part of the eternal now. Just look at the Dalai Lama, who goes around constantly laughing and giggling. I don't know whether Mr. Lama is in love at the moment, but I know he is extremely intimate with the present moment.

Beauty from laughter

When you laugh, your face, your body, and your whole personality become more open. You become more extroverted and more obliging. You show that you are happy and that you are able to enjoy life. Laughter increases the blood flow to the fine blood capillaries in your skin. Your skin becomes warmer and you begin to glow, which makes you more attractive. Laughter is a sign of wellbeing and surplus energy, calmness and confidence. Happy, laughing people are pleasant to be with.

Royal laughter

Simple feelings of affection and warmth can be conveyed via laughter. You should see what happens when the press is interviewing the Danish Queen, Margrethe II. This often takes place at her husband, Prince Henrik's, castle in Southern France. Margrethe is there on holiday with her husband and the dachshund dogs, Rolf and Dolfi, who know their place at the royal feet. On the sunny terrace at Cahors, tall Danish press photographers and journalists cast shadows on the walls of the ancient château. Queen Margrethe is in good spirits and ready to answer all the questions, although she already knows what she is going to be asked.

No matter how trivial the question, the Queen's answer never fails to spread warm and genuine laughter throughout the gathered press. The Queen doesn't say anything particularly funny; she simply answers the questions. Yet it makes the press laugh. Why? Because the Danes adore their queen. They want to show their respect and affection for Margrethe and they show this respect and affection by laughing when she talks glowingly about her son Prince Frederik and his wife, Princess Mary.

I have to admit though, that I mostly laugh because I am reminded of a Danish comedian, Preben Christensen, who does the most wonderful impersonation of the Danish queen.

Exercise: Royal laughter

Wave your hand like the Queen (you can pick any queen you want – the Danish Queen, the English Queen, or any other queen!) would, while passing in her carriage. Laugh in a light and cultivated manner. You'll soon find that real laughter takes over!

CHAPTER #4

4.3
Why we laugh: To live in the moment, worry less and deal with difficult times

> I, not events, have the power to make me happy or unhappy today. I can choose which it shall be. Yesterday is dead, tomorrow hasn't arrived yet. I have just one day, today, and I'm going to be happy in it.
> - Groucho Marx, Writings For By And About Groucho Marx

Happy lemons

I guess what I want to tell you the most is this: life will never be perfect. We can't make everything go our way. People will still do bad things and disasters will still happen. But we can take control of how we respond to this, and we can take control of our own happiness.

When life gives you lemons, laughter can help you make them happy lemons.

Laughter and the present moment

Laughter is your ticket to the present moment. When you laugh, you are rooted in the present. It is not possible to think whilst you are laughing, and therefore, laughter is a direct entrance into the here and now. When you are fully present, you can feel yourself here and now. You are in your body. You can really sense and enjoy life right now. If you want more laughter in your life, you must search for and be in the present moment.

The way we live is very much guided by thoughts of tomorrow, with our thoughts overruling our feelings. We often forget that we should be there for each other right now. Many of us are controlled by our wishes and expectations for the future. The brain is treated solely as an amazing tool for designing the life we want...at some point in the future! Many of us forget the present moment. It is now that your life is actually being lived! Putting it bluntly, if you are not here in the moment, then you are not living!

Exercise: Check back in to the moment

The mind has a habit of constantly checking out of the moment. Often we check out of the present to think about things that we need to do in the future, or things we should have done differently in the past. Nothing wrong with that in moderation, but if your mind is always flying back and forth between the past and the future, it doesn't leave you much space to enjoy now, and can affect your happiness and drain away your laughter.

Start becoming aware of how often you check out of the moment each day. Then follow these instructions to check back into the moment regularly.

- When you get to work, take five conscious deep breaths.
- When your first cup of coffee or tea is in front of you in the morning,

sit and take some conscious deep breaths.
- When you are talking to your friends or family next, practise really listening to them consciously – not preparing what you are about to say but really listening to them, and filling yourself with what they are saying.
- The next meal you eat, really notice the texture and flavour of everything in your mouth. Allow yourself to savour it and immerse yourself in the sensations of it.
- When you walk down the street, feel the sensation of your feet on the ground as you move – feel where your clothing touches your body, and the wind on your skin.

At the moment, we are witnessing a rapid growth in the establishment of yoga centres, meditation courses, tai-chi workshops and so on. All of them have one purpose: to teach us to let go of our thoughts. Thoughts control our lives to such a great degree that many of us are not aware of what we are actually feeling in this moment.

What are you feeling right now? Are you living the life you want to live, or do you need to make some changes in order to get more out of life? The time machine has already been invented. It sits in your skull and goes by the name of 'the brain'. If you are like most people, then you probably spend most of your life in this time machine. The brain is a fantastic tool, but if you are completely controlled by it, instead of taking control, then you most probably spend a lot of time on fear and worrying about the future.

It sounds counter-intuitive, but being present in the moment can really help you to cope if you have a difficult life, or a life you are not happy with. It sounds like being more present in your difficult life would make it seem worse, but being able to live in the present moment can help you to let go of worries about the future and regrets about the past, and focus only on the problems in front of you. If you can just focus on what you have to deal with right here and now, you will have more mental resources to concentrate on the practical things you need to do in order to turn your life into something you don't just have to tolerate. This might mean you become able to see your problems more clearly, and figure out a way to get help to solve them, or it might mean that you can focus more clearly on a way to get from where you are now to the place you want to be in the goals you imagine for yourself.

Exercise: Mindfulness meditation

This exercise is a good start to becoming more present in the moment.

Allow yourself 10 minutes every day for a week (a lot of people find it gives them lots of energy to do this in the morning). Switch off your mobile phone and the radio and try and exclude any other source of noise – it doesn't have to be totally silent but it will help you concentrate to start with if you can remove possible distractions.

Sit down in a comfortable position and resolve that this is time you are taking just for yourself. Feel and become aware of your breath. You breathe in and you breathe out again. Take a few minutes to establish a good breathing rhythm. Feel your heartbeat. Feel your heartbeat and experience that you are your heart. Imagine that you are looking at the activity occurring in your brain from a position in your heart. You are your heart. Observe your thoughts from this place. Notice what kind of thoughts come and go in your mind. Sit in your heart and observe your thoughts in this way for ten minutes.

When you have done this exercise every day for a week, you will achieve a different level of consciousness. You will experience that you have become able to view your thoughts from outside. Thus, you will become conscious that you are not your brain's activity. You will notice that a great many thoughts pass through your mind that you actually have no need for. This will give you the ability to acknowledge and let go of those thoughts concerned with everyday anxieties, worries and negativity – thoughts that are often unfounded.

When you do this exercise and you experience thoughts in your brain that do not contribute positively to your life, then let them pass by, don't give them your attention. Every time some useless negativity arises in your mind, let it pass by. Don't try not to think about them (or you will find you can think of nothing else!), just tell yourself that you don't need to think of that now, and let the thought flow away. Eventually, you will be able to get into the habit of managing your mind, so that you can transfer this ability into your everyday life and control your helpful and less helpful thoughts. In the present moment, we can experience happiness, freedom and intimacy. It is our thoughts about the future which cause us the biggest problems. Just stop and think a moment about how many of your worries never actually came true. Think about all the hundreds of hours that you spent imagining unpleasant and fearful things that might happen, which never actually happened.

Even if your worries are going to come true (or have come true in the past), there is no sense wasting the present moment on fear and worry – if you are able to let go of your worries about the future and participate more fully in the present moment, you will have greater mental energy for doing something about the future, and making plans to improve your life. You will also have greater mental resources for caring for yourself and your loved ones.

Be conscious in the present moment

The more conscious you are in the present moment, the better you will be at making the right decisions. When you are truly present, you will sense and feel what is right for you right now. Life is one long 'now', so it makes perfect sense to direct all your energy into the present moment. Many people have their focus placed way too far out into the future. Of course, it is necessary to look into the future now and then, just as long as it doesn't become a habitual state of mind. Personally, I have set myself four or five goals, wishes or aims for the future, but I am very conscious about working on these goals in the present moment. I enjoy thinking about these goals a couple of times during the day, and I think about the pleasure I experience by just being on my way towards them. When I feel the energy these aims will bring me once I've accomplished them, the joy of the journey is doubled.

The less conscious you are in the moment the more you will make "wrong" choices. If you are not directing your attention to the moment then you won't be aware of your feelings here and now. A journey of a thousand miles starts with a single step, and each step has a particular meaning for you. With each step along the way, you will learn about, feel and notice the nature of your life, building your identity and life experiences upon this. If you consider your steps insignificant, then your life will be insignificant. If you find you fall foul of circumstance, or make the wrong decision, you will find yourself out on one of life's small detours. Perhaps no decision is really wrong, for even a wrong choice will serve the important purpose of showing you what you *don't* want in your life. Some people make many, many small detours. They walk on and on until it hurts so much, they just have to turn around.

Others live their entire lives in pain – oblivious to the possibility of making fresh choices. In their minds there exists only one possibility, only one choice. The good news is that you will be offered thousands of chances in this life. At the appearance of every new moment, you have the chance of something different.

Exercise: The journey of a thousand miles starts with a single step

Go down to you local toy store and buy a little blackboard and some chalk. Put it up in your living room, your kitchen or your bedroom.

List three things that you wish for in your life. Under this, write a small and practical way in which you can get closer to each one.

Look at the board every day and be conscious about taking steps towards your fantastic life. (When you complete the steps – which you will! – you can rub them out and write new ones.)

Positive and negative control

Every human quality contains the potential for good. In the same way, every human quality holds the potential for bad. "All things in moderation" is an excellent guideline for regulating our behaviour and ensuring our wellbeing. Everything we use to excess - whether it's food, wine, cigarettes, sport, sex, anger or something else - can rebound and hit us in the neck like a boomerang.

It's good to be able to exercise self-discipline. But if you think that you can steer and control everything around you, then I am certain that you are generally not having much of a good time. It is an impossible task you are trying to achieve. You will never – not in your wildest dreams – have the chance to fully control anyone but yourself. The world is constantly changing. You are constantly changing. The people around you are constantly changing. And this includes both negative and positive change. Nothing and no one remains constant. Everything is moving, growing and dying. When you can accept this, that nothing is permanent, and that everything is changing, you can perhaps also accept that nothing will fit into your fixed frame. Even your frame is actually constantly growing and changing.

If your happiness is dependent on other people and the world behaving in a particular way (your way), you will never feel calm inside. The only thing you should wish for is the ability to be able to control yourself. The only way to have genuine control is to let go of all the things you wish to control, because control is just the brain's illusion that everything is predictable. The present moment is always different from the 'now' you thought would happen. The outer world always reacts differently than we had expected. Trying to form a 'now' that will perform as we wanted is an impossible task.

By letting go of that idea, we can return our focus to the present moment. By letting go we can empower ourselves to deal with what is right in front of us.

What is realistic?

You probably know people who will tell you that you have to be realistic. These are usually family and friends, sensible people, who seem to know just what is best for you. But what is best for you and what is realistic? Realism means remaining in the bounds of reality. Or for those who use the word in this way – within the bounds of what they think is possible. 400 years ago, people believed the sun went round the earth. At that time in history, it was reality. If you were silly enough to suggest that things might be different, you would find yourself on trial for heresy, like poor Galileo.

What seems real to you can seem quite unreal to others, and what is impossible for you can be simple and easy for others. So when we tell other people what we believe to be possible, we are normally making such judgments from a standpoint of what is possible for us; our own personal laws of nature. To put this in another, rather more negative, way: we tend to assume that those around us share our own limitations. Often when others tell you what they think is best for you, they are actually telling you what they think is best or right for themselves.

> We don't see things as they are, we see things as we are.
>
> - Anais Nin

The times in your life where you make exactly the right choices for you, you might remember as the times you acted in total accordance with the possibilities available in the present, along with that wonderful feeling of 'rightness' that flashed through your body in exactly that moment. It is said that intuition is the soul whispering to you between two thoughts.

Intuition is the voice within you that often has the right answer. You probably have lots of examples from your own life of times when you have made what you felt was a rational decision; some situation in which you had been told by parents, friends or your own brain, that you had to be realistic and do the 'right thing'. You listened to common sense, to logic, only to later discover, that you had made the wrong choice for you. Then you remember that there was a voice inside you that had told you to do something different. Being rooted in the present will allow you access to this voice thereby enabling you to better realise the best option for you right now.

Finding your own truth in the present moment

When you are intimately present in the here-and-now, you have the chance to discover deeper meaning in your life. In the present moment you can come into complete accord with your own deepest values, and be able to find out what is really important to you. You will be able to know your own truth.

Maybe the ultimate meaning of your existence is not apparent to you today. But taking a series of small decisions that are right for you will eventually lead you onto a path where life will flow more easily.

Exercise: Value check

You can care for yourself and others in the best way, and make the best decisions for you, when you act in a way that is aligned with your most important values. Follow this value check exercise to keep yourself conscious of what is really important to you, and to help you reflect your values in your actions.

Write down ten things that you feel are really important values to you. Put up this list somewhere prominent in your house. After a few days, narrow the list down to five values. Then after a few more days, narrow it down again to the two or three that you feel are the most important to you. Make a promise to yourself that you will stay true to these values that really matter to you.

Here's a list of values to get you started – don't stick to this list though but be sure to use any that matter to you:

Assertiveness, caring, commitment, compassion, confidence, consideration, cooperation, courage, courtesy, creativity, determination, diligence, enthusiasm, flexibility, forgiveness, friendliness, generosity, gentleness, helpfulness, honour, humility, idealism, integrity, joyfulness, justice, kindness, love, loyalty, moderation, modesty, orderliness, patience, peacefulness, perseverance, purposefulness, reliability, respect, responsibility, self-discipline, service, tact, thankfulness, tolerance, trust, trustworthiness, truthfulness, understanding, unity.

I have found many paths to the present moment. The present is a place where I am in complete balance, peace and accord with all that exists in that moment. I am here, without being my past or my future, present to all other life, just now. I am aware of my pulse; I can feel the pulse of all life on earth – animals, plants and other human beings.

A time when I really access the present moment is when I ride my motorcycle on long trips on the highways. When I have driven for a while, left the city behind and have come out onto the wide expanses of the open road, something happens. A connection arises between me and my motorbike. On the highway there are no mobile phones, no car radios, no coffee or tea to spill in my lap. Here, there is only myself, 700cc and the horizon.

I ride a chopper, which has an engine that sounds like a fishing boat. After riding for some time, my thoughts begin to melt away, words disappear and my sensory impressions become much stronger. The shifting smells from the natural world around me become a part of my body and my breath. The wind on my cheeks makes my face relax. The thudding of the engine becomes one with my body, the pulse of the motorbike becomes my pulse, my heartbeat becomes its heartbeat. There arises a sensual trinity between nature, the earth and me. Everything is one and on the same frequency. On the road to Skanderborg I felt that I became a part of an almost divine picture. It was here that I felt and saw how everything is connected.

It was early evening and the sun hung, mild and round, casting shades of pink across the beautiful evening sky. I suddenly saw how everything was bound together by love. I saw how everything lived and grew from love. I saw that deep down, every animal, plant and human just wants love. I saw, felt and experienced that life is very simple. We live for love and we die in its absence. Everyone wants to love – everyone – and it is only our egos that limit our potential for love. The heart is full of love and the heart has unlimited supplies of love to give.

In reality, everybody has understood the meaning of life. Everyone is hunting for love, looking for it in some form or another. Instinctively, we know that it is here – in love itself – that we will find meaning. Within true unconditional love lies peace, harmony and balance. Here is the place where paradise on earth exists. When we are together with another person, giving and receiving unconditional love, we experience a childlike lightness and happiness that can make us laugh without any reason.

When adults communicate with adults, we move up into our minds. Therefore, a lot of adult communication goes wrong. Fear breeds fear, distrust leads to distrust and worries just produce more worries. If we want to change this world, then we have to focus on that which is the most important in this world: love! We have to learn to listen to our hearts. We should communicate to both adults and children from our hearts. Start with your heart right now – here lies truth and the meaning of it all.

My own laughter club

One of my greatest experiences, not just in terms of laughter, was when I opened my own laughter club: Allerød Laughter Club.

I had been greatly inspired by Østerbro Laughter Club, the first laughter club to be founded in Denmark. What made it special was that the meetings were held in someone's private home. The other clubs in Denmark provided great opportunities to laugh, but yet, being invited into the warmth of someone's home was far more cosy than meeting in public. Another aspect that was important to me, was the value of being open, which is much easier to be in a private home. When you are open, you can truly absorb and feel how things are. Openness also creates trust and contact to other people on a deeper level. So, having decided that I wanted to open my own laughter club, there was no doubt in my mind that it should be in my own home.

The week before, the local newspaper carried a full-page feature covering the opening night of Allerød Laughter Club - an event which was to be held in my very own front room. On that evening, and subsequent evenings, anyone was welcome to participate free of charge. On our opening night, Doctor Madan Kataria, founder of the world laughter yoga movement, was our guest of honour, bringing with him his bright laughter and words of wisdom.

From the very beginning, I had a really good feeling about this new venture and this feeling was confirmed on the very first night, when around 50 local people turned up in my front room. Fantastic. Witnessing so many 'strangers' making themselves at home in my living room was a completely unique experience. The trust and openness that I was offering was returned by expressions of gratitude, humility and happiness from these new friends. The laughter club was off to a magnificent start. Following on from this, I held a session of the laughter club every other Wednesday at 7:30 p.m. Every fortnight, a notice in the local newspaper announced that the doors of Thomas Flindt's home would be open for laughter once again – and that it was free. After a couple of months, a group of about 15-20 people had stabilised. Of course, new people turned every time, but from the start, a core group was established who still come to all of the club's sessions.

After three months, I asked these people what it meant to them to be able to come and practice group laughter twice monthly. Everyone answered that there was now more laughter in their lives, and not just in the forum of the club. When they experienced something funny, they felt that they could now laugh more resoundingly and freely than they had previously allowed themselves to do. Several answered that they were also less worried about what others thought when they laughed out loud in public. This lack of concern had spread to other areas of their lives.

Many of the participants had simply stopped worrying as much. They felt that they could live in the moment more easily and were less anxious about the future. When we laugh, we are free of worries for a short time, simply because it is impossible to think about things while we are laughing. If we can laugh more than momentarily, then we can be free of concerns more than momentarily.

It makes me extremely proud to know that I can help people bring more joy into their lives. After a couple of months, I could see that the club had a strongly therapeutic effect. After just 4-6 sessions, the participants had simply become better at enjoying life. Amazing.

CHAPTER #4

4.4
Why we laugh:
To release tension and stress

Relieving stress with laughter

70% of all illnesses prevalent in the Western world are stress-related. Now, just hang on a minute - what is actually going on in our world right now?

Our minds have run away from us – out into the future trying to solve all kinds of problems – while our bodies wither away in the present.

However, when we laugh we release stress, tension and pain. Scientific research has shown that laughter causes our muscles to relax and relieves pain under hard physical duress or sickness. The late Dr Annette Goodheart, worked with laughter therapy for over 30 years. Goodheart's theory was this: we don't laugh because it is fun, we laugh to release tension - but it is fun to laugh.

No doubt everybody believes that they have a natural and healthy relationship with laughter. We all know when it is appropriate to laugh and when it is inappropriate to do so. Most people laugh when they are having fun, when they are being entertained or when they find themselves in situations bubbling with positive feelings. But we know now that laughter can also help us to relieve and release stress, tension and pain.

If you want to learn something new about life, and at the same time, to release masses of energy, then consider laughing at something which is actually not funny at all – such as your stress, your tension and your pain.

One of the reasons we don't laugh that much as adults, is because we're often tensed up, stressed or in pain. Yet, this might be precisely where the key to your laughter lies. In Dr Goodheart's therapy and with other laughter therapists, the idea is to laugh your tension and stress and pain away. She has had a great deal of success with laughter therapy over the past 30 years.

In laughter therapy sessions you are personally guided into your tension, stress and pain and asked to describe its source. When your coach has understood the nature of your problem, he or she will invite you into a process whereby you get a chance to see your stress, tension and pain from a different perspective. Your coach will ask you whether you would like to laugh at it. When you are sitting with a laughter coach, you will probably say yes to such an invitation. The coach will then formulate a few sentences focusing on your problem which you will be asked to repeat and finish off with a "tee hee" or a "hee hee" or a "ho ho". If you have had a good process with your coach, you will with all probability end by laughing your body free of your tension.

Most laughter coaches have worked with laughter for many years and when your laughter first breaks through you will find yourself sitting with someone who wants to laugh along with you.

"Those of us who have laughed until we've cried know that in the middle of the process, we can't tell which is which. We do not laugh because we are happy and cry because we're sad – we laugh or cry because we have tension, stress, or pain. Laughter and tears rebalance the chemicals our body create when these distressed states are present, and so we feel better after we have laughed or cried".

- Annette Goodheart, Laughter Therapy

Stress and the present moment

A few hundred years ago, most of us worked on the land. At that time, most people used their bodies fully. Much of this work was characterised by routine and did not demand much in the way of mental effort. In other words, the brain could relax as the body worked. Today our situation is completely the opposite. Many of us have undertaken long periods of academic study and are highly trained in using our mental capacities to make a living.

Businesses today demand great flexibility. Products and ideas develop at such great speed, that we need to be able to think into the future to survive. It's good to be able to plan and direct our attention towards the future, but the problems arise when we forget ourselves in the present. If we don't return to the here and now when we have finished work, then we actually never stop working. When you leave work in the evening, you normally switch off your computer. But do you give your brain a chance to rest when the day's work is done?

You are your thoughts, your mental life, but you are much, much more than this. You are your body, your spirit and your soul. You are your heart. Your body has communicated with you for many years. Many times you have not listened and you have either become sick or something else mysterious has happened in your life. Your heart also talks to you.

The heart beats in your body in the present moment - with every feeling you have, in every moment you have. Your heart tries to communicate with you too.

Your brain is often out travelling in time. It is your brain that stresses you all the time with its constant reminders of the tasks of tomorrow. It is also your brain that keeps you from the present moment and life's true essence: laughter, the joy of life and love. Try closing this book for a moment. Try to sit for a minute and observe your thoughts. Notice how many of these thoughts have nothing to do with what is happening now. Notice how the mind deserts the moment constantly.

Exercise: Be mindful in your daily life

Being mindful means having an observant mind, which is free from worry and conflict. It doesn't mean that you will never experience conflict or worry again – it simply means that you don't approach people or situations with a conflicted or worried mind.

Don't put pressure on yourself while you practise this exercise – just approach it in a spirit of calm and playfulness.

Decide to have a mindful mind for one day. Shift your consciousness – observe what is happening in your life before you think or react. For one day, observe everything in both your inner and outer world. Just observe it – don't jump to any fast conclusions about situations, about yourself or about other people. Just observe everything that comes at you without attaching a meaning to it. Give your mind the freedom to observe without tension. You will find that many things that you are worrying about ebb away when following this practice.

The reward that lies in being able to access the moment is that stress is reduced, and everything is experienced more intensely. Positive experiences - a conversation, a sunset, a hug, eroticism, the weather, time spent with your children - are all experienced much more powerfully than before, because you are much more present in what is now. Negative experiences are therefore also experienced more intensely, which is positive in the respect that we are able to truly feel if something influences us, and thus react more quickly to it. By being present in the moment, when we have a negative experience, we can stop negative thoughts from taking hold, and focus on changing our circumstances for the better, simply because we don't let them take control.

Netkoncept Laughter

The sales department of a large Danish computer company, Netkoncept, had been suffering a period of uncertainty and considerable upheaval. The sales manager, Lasse Christensen, believed that the staff were in need of some pampering and fun. Lasse rang me and asked for a course of morning laughter for the whole department (around 50 sales people) ASAP!

And so it was that on Tuesday, August 16th 2005 I started a 14-day morning laughter course with the sales department at Netkoncept.

All the young sales reps gathered that Tuesday morning in the canteen, where I introduced them to the concept and the course we were about to embark upon. I told them that group laughter has a therapeutic effect, that it opens the mind and helps us to access even deeper levels of laughter. I told them that I was very interested in the effects of group laughter and that I was constantly looking to document and understand these effects. I asked whether there might be two or three volunteers amongst them, who would be willing to write a diary charting the process, describing any effects experienced as a result of participating. I told them that it did not matter what their attitude to the project was – whether they were sceptical or enthusiastic made no difference. The only thing that was necessary was a willingness to write a diary over the next fortnight.

Laughter diary

Two men, Christian Schwarts-Sørensen and Jacob Rentsch Larsen, raised their hands. "I'd like to do that", they both said. After the introduction and the first laughter session, I sat down to talk to Christian and Jacob. I told them that I wanted them to write things in their own way, but that it would be great if they could answer the following questions each day:

How were you feeling before you laughed today?
What happened inside you when we began laughing?
What happened between you and your colleagues as you were laughing?
What happened in the rest of the working day?
What happened after you left work?
Has anything changed in your private life?

What was interesting about reading Christian and Jacob's diaries was how rapidly laughter appeared to influence their state of mind, improving their mood and leading to greater motivation. The practice of group laughter appeared to create a new form of contact between colleagues. Christian suddenly began to see the people around him in a completely new light. He also experienced that he was perceived in a new and more positive way. Jacob noticed he had greater mental energy and that he was significantly less stressed during and after the course. Here follows a selection of entries from their diaries.

The diary of Christian Schwarts-Sørensen:

August 16th, 2005

I had a really bad morning, was feeling negative about life and mentally distant after my return from three weeks' holiday. I found it hard to be enthusiastic due to this post-holiday depression, but laughed along and began to feel warmth and happiness spreading throughout my body. My state of mind was lifted to a noticeably higher level. The atmosphere became lighter as more and more of us began to smile. People began to laugh, also unmotivated. The rest of the day I was more at ease and felt much more enthusiastic about dealing with the day's assignments compared to the previous day, when I had been really down in the dumps. I was more open and communicative because my state of mind had improved. People smiled more today.

August 17th, 2005

I had a significantly better morning - not so down about life anymore, but back to my normal self. I could feel the enthusiasm from the day before still simmering just below the surface. I felt a little shy as we began to laugh, although this quickly disappeared again after a couple of minutes' laughter as the familiar warm bubbles began to spread through my body. I wasn't focused on my colleagues so much, but had my attention directed inward, focusing on my own level of openness. During the free laughter, I noticed that I could activate and magnify other people's laughter with my own. For the rest of the day, I found myself chuckling and smiling without any particular reason…. Has anything changed in your private life? Well, I keep catching myself smiling and chuckling when I think back to today's laughter session, and my girlfriend says I'm not as bad-tempered as I usually am.

August 19th, 2005

I slept wonderfully and felt really on top of things in terms of wellbeing and mental energy. I had a fit of the giggles just as I was lying there trying to get off to sleep when I remembered one of the previous laughter sessions. What happened inside you when we began laughing? Once I started, I just couldn't stop - it had a runaway effect, like an exponential equation, exploding in power. I found it liberating to let go and release all my tension in such an uplifting manner. I couldn't stop again because the others sat chortling away, which resulted in an upward spiral of laughter…It is as though a black cloud of tension and pressure above the sales department is dispersing, as the atmosphere becomes more friendly and jovial. … I feel like I have more physical and mental energy and, in many situations, I am managing to view things in a more positive and optimistic light.

August 25th, 2005
I am laughing more and more without having any particular reason, or because others' laughter sets me off and then I cannot stop. It feels like invisible boundaries are being dissolved and we are getting closer to each other than before. For me, personally, I feel a greater desire to be sociable and to communicate with my colleagues. I am now exchanging comments with colleagues I had previously not spoken to.

August 26th, 2005
... The working day is still the same length, but time seems to pass more quickly when we have laughed together; time flies by and suddenly it is time to go home. I now pass colleagues in the corridor and smile at them and then we are off, laughing without reason – it is completely fantastic. Has anything changed in your private life? I have shifted some personal boundaries. Being able to open up in other people's company and really engage myself, to fool around more and show my silly side, running the risk that I might look like a complete idiot, has had the effect of giving me substantially greater courage to start up conversations or engage with others than I had before. This is primarily with people I have previously not spoken to or have had a limited amount of contact with. If I manage to have the courage to laugh out loud right in the middle of a group of people, then basically there are no limits to what I am capable of.

The diary of Jacob Rentsch Larsen:

August 22nd, 2005
A few people have begun to really invest themselves and let go of their inhibitions. This has had an effect throughout the entire group – with people laughing at those lying on the floor already dissolved in laughter. Great effect! We have begun to look around and establish eye contact with each other, which also has a catalytic effect on the laughter. Meeting each other in the corridor throughout the day, many of us will laugh out loud, as if to affirm membership of the laughter club. What is more, we have begun to laugh spontaneously during our internal meetings. Didn't feel as though I had had a stressful day today – but did not as-

sume this was a result of the laughter course. I realised at some point, that I didn't have control over a particular situation – but instead of working against that feeling, I just let go, which was unbelievably helpful and rewarding. I am feeling energetic and motivated, and look forward to coming to work each morning.

August 24th, 2005

Many of my colleagues have now begun to laugh without being 'instructed' to… I can clearly feel that a community has arisen across the different departments of the sales organisation and that the laughter club has established a sense of solidarity amongst us. New bonds have been forged and I feel that I have become closer to both my staff and my colleagues. I felt that my daily 'stress level' had fallen significantly and that I had more mental energy. Began to wonder whether it was the laughter course that was leading to these effects – but quickly dismissed the thought.

August 26th, 2005

I can feel I have greater physical energy and a happiness that I cannot explain, other than having something to do with participating in the laughter course. No other aspects of my life have changed – and therefore, I am now convinced that it is the laughter that has caused these effects.

I discussed my experiences with my colleagues and several of them had experienced the same thing. We laughed and said to each other that we should continue the course and even form a laughter club both inside and outside of the workplace. Things have generally improved socially and this benefits our cooperation in several areas. Amongst other things, we are now better at small talk and also at asking each other how things are going. Of course, this is also easier when one feels one has got to know each other better.

Generally, I feel physically much better. Especially stress at work has the tendency to wear me out and take all my surplus energy, which means that when I come home, I am often completely drained. This has not been the case during the recent period – and I have been able to leave my work behind when I went home. If we can keep up this trend, then it is my strong conviction that we can avoid stress and prevent burnout amongst management and workers! ... My girlfriend has also noticed that I have given her more attention, in addition to having the resources to become engaged with other things than just those related to work and practical duties.

In other words, you could say that I have become better at living in the moment, that I have become more present. ... Personally, I have felt a huge difference in both my private and professional life.

Positive and negative forms of tension

Tension appears in many different forms. There are both positive and negative forms of tension. Everyone knows the experience of holding tension in the body and it can even be the cause of laughter. Here are a few examples:

Positive tension could be:

- The moment a comedian delivers their punch line
- When the final lotto number rolls out the tube of that enigmatically-designed machine
- When your physics teacher gives you an a-grade in your final exam
- When you open that christmas present you really wanted
- When your child says 'mommy' or 'daddy' for the first time

Negative tension might come in the form of:

- Your neighbour's wild and unkempt hedge
- An unresolved conflict with your partner
- A tense relationship with your boss

- Too much work
- Not enough fun

Look at the above examples and then try and play with the following thought: what would happen if you had a really good laugh with your neighbour? I mean the neighbour that can't seem to get their act together to trim the hedge. Don't you think it would be a lot easier to make an agreement about cutting it after sharing some moments of hilarity? My guess is that it would be MUCH easier. After a good chortle, you and your neighbour will be much more relaxed. You will have let go of all negative thoughts about each other - and the hedge. You will have cleansed your minds and found a suitable outlet for all that pent-up tension. You might even be so calm and relaxed, that you will be able to laugh at the terrible state of the hedge. Laughter makes communicating difficult things easier, and can be used to smooth the roughest paths between people in life.

In films, they tend to make fun of tension, stress and pain. Talented filmmakers know the art of taking simple, everyday situations and projecting them in such way that we might see ourselves and our own problems reflected in them. When we watch films, we may find ourselves laughing at the tension, the stress or the pain that actually exists in our own lives. Has the time come where you and I can begin to laugh at the problems and pain we are currently experiencing in our lives?

After meeting Annette Goodheart, it became clear to me that laughter and tears had a much greater significance than I had realised. Was this knowledge new, or had we always known it deep down inside? I asked my good friend, the theatre director Veronika Kær, what she thought about this. Veronika is one of the most talented and well-known directors in Danish theatre. With countless plays and performances behind her, including classics like *Blood Wedding* and *1001 Nights*, she is also very much in the business of laughter and tears. I therefore asked Veronika to write something about the theatre's perspective on these aspects of human existence.

Veronika answered me poetically, scientifically and historically:

Catharsis means to let it out, to let oneself be led into and be present in a purification process. Indeed, I would claim… that catharsis was the true measurement for both comedy and tragedy. It was more about purification than art.

Around 400 BC, the Greeks were working with theatre as a method of eliciting a purification process. The audience, the actors, the playwright and the producer all knew that the theatre's greatest task was to bring about catharsis. To tell a hilarious story of intense comedy or an impressive myth filled with deep tragedy, had the very same purpose. *Catharsis!* Everyone present in the art form, players and audience, were led into and through this purification process. By influencing and letting oneself be influenced, by being receptive to collective exchange, a chemical and mental process could manifest, which caused everyone to leave the theatre feeling physically healthier and more mentally clarified as individuals. It didn't really matter whether it was tears or laughter which had taken one to this state. It was mainly a question of synergy. In this regard, I find it very thought-provoking to observe the current value attributed to theatre by this society.

What is art, or even life, worth if we don't let ourselves be influenced by or influence others, and for this sphere of mutual influence to embrace both the sharing of happiness and sorrow?

We say in the trade that, 'Theatre cannot stand alone'. Unfortunately however, we are so concerned with developing our individual professional skills or finding the next job, that we completely forget our true assignment: to influence others. On the other hand, this is not an easy task, when the audience is reluctant to allow itself to be influenced. We need to think about that. I would encourage you, the reader of these words, to dare express what you experience, when you next find yourself sitting in a theatre. We players need this in order to give you what you need. To allow yourself to be touched and influenced feeds a reaction, which in turn feeds another reaction - and in this way, we create communication, synergy and community.

-Veronika Kær

Laughter, tears and anger are just waves of energy that have a specific purpose - to course through the body like a storm, a wave of happiness or a downpour of rain to then leave the body once again.

Imbalance arises because we don't really allow such processes to take place in our bodies. We resist and we suppress our laughter, tears and anger. Imbalance is quite simply the result of unreleased happiness, anger and sorrow.

Be your own laughter guru and let go of stress and tension

Now it's your turn to be your own laughter guru. In this exercise, you will use your laughter to develop more laughter and to release tension.

Exercise: Laugh at your problems

Remember that if this is too uncomfortable for you to do, stop the exercise and don't push yourself. Think of something that has been worrying you, and try to think of as many ridiculous things about the situation or the problem as you can. Now try laughing at it, to release the stress and tension you have built up through worrying about it. It sounds crazy, but if you manage it, you should be able to take away the situation or problem's power to worry you, and develop the habit of laughing away your stress about it.

This may be too difficult, as you may feel too worried or stressed to laugh at your problems without feeling upset – and that's OK too.

Laugh at your mistakes to forgive yourself

I have known that laughter contains forgiveness for some time now. I found this out one morning, when I knocked my bowl of cornflakes and milk onto the floor and onto my brand new suede shoes (only 5 minutes before I had to leave the house). It struck me that if I could laugh at myself in this situation, then I could also forgive myself. I pointed at the mess of cornflakes and the milk, which was slowly seeping into my shoes, and laughed at myself - albeit in a somewhat strained way. All habits are conditioned. I decided to make a habit of laughing at myself every time I made a blunder. I decided that I would point at the mistake and then at myself and simply laugh. At the start (and still, in some of the more difficult situations) this came out as a couple of half-hearted and unconvincing "ha has", whilst forcing my face into a huge grin. But after a while, as I became better and better at saying "ha ha" or "hee hee", when I made a mistake, I realised how ridiculous it actually is to tell ourselves off. Getting angry with yourself cannot put any mistake right (as my cornflake experience shows, it really is no use crying over spilt milk!). Forgive yourself and regard the situation from a fresh perspective. Today, after many, many blunders, I can truly laugh spontaneously when I mess things up...

Exercise: Laugh at your mistakes

Try this for a whole day if you can. Next time you make a mistake, point at the mistake and say, "Ha ha ha". Remember to smile when you say this. You can also point at the mistake and yourself at the same time as you laugh. Repeat this many times, so that it becomes an entertaining habit. It can feel quite difficult and maybe a little provocative to laugh at your mistakes, but you will be pleasantly surprised (and a little relieved) the day when you begin to laugh voluntarily at the small mistakes you happen to make.

Once you have learned to laugh at your mistakes and stop punishing yourself mentally each time you make one, you will have achieved a far more relaxed attitude to yourself. People around you will also become more relaxed in your company and you will be guaranteed to bring more laughter into your life.

Fake it until you make it

It might seem a bit difficult to make the decision to laugh when you're feeling stressed, upset, afraid, or embarrassed, and it's the last thing you feel like doing, but intentional laughter builds your laughter muscles, so to speak, and makes it easier to access your genuine laughter and all its benefits. It's like how you might not enjoy the long, hard training runs in the cold and rain, but on the day of the marathon you will feel the benefit of the effort that you put in, as you cross the finishing line with ease.

In this way, we make a choice to help our laughter along the way, much like push-starting a car. You need to invest some energy at the start, you cough and splutter for a while with the effort, but then suddenly, your 'engine' engages and off you go... your body wants to laugh! The body loves when it is tuned into the frequency of laughter. At the end of the day, I don't think your body is in the least bit concerned whether it is a joke or something else that has started you off. The body just loves to laugh, which is pretty easy to understand when you think of all the wonderful health benefits laughter brings with it.

Exercise: The food of love

Eating something delicious is a good way to relieve your stress (and dark chocolate stimulates the production of your body's natural mood-elevators and painkillers- just like laughter does - has antioxidant properties, and lowers your blood pressure) and baking can be very relaxing. It might sound weird to put aubergine in a cake, but take a leap into the unknown and you won't be disappointed.
Bake this and share it with someone you like or someone you love. I

guarantee it will put a smile on their face (especially when they find out what's in it)!

Sugar free aubergine chocolate cake

Ingredients:

2 small aubergines (weighing about 400g / 1lb)
300g / 10.5oz high quality dark chocolate (minimum 70% cocoa solids), broken into small pieces
50g / 2oz high quality cocoa powder
60g / 2.5oz ground almonds
3 medium eggs
200g / 7oz clear honey
2 tsp baking powder
1/4 tsp salt
1 tbsp brandy (optional)

Method:

1. Preheat the oven to 180°C / 350°F. Line a 9"/23cm loose bottomed tin with baking parchment and lightly oil the base and sides.

2. Prick the aubergines all over with a skewer, then place in a bowl covered in cling film. Microwave on high for 8 minutes until they are cooked and limp. Discard any water at the bottom. Leave to stand until they are cool enough to handle (but don't let them get cold).

3. Skin the aubergines and puree in a blender. Once the aubergine is pureed and smooth, add the chocolate, which should melt slowly. Cover the bowl with clingfilm and set aside until all the chocolate has melted.

4. In a large bowl, whisk up all the other ingredients until well mixed and slightly bubbly. Fold the melted chocolate and aubergine mixture into the bowl with all the other ingredients.

5. Pour the mixture into the prepared tin and cook in the bottom of the oven for 30 minutes.

6. Remove the cake from the oven and let it cool in the tin for 15 minutes before turning it out onto a wire rack and peeling off the baking parchment. Quickly turn it the right way up again and set it on a plate.

7. Sieve some cocoa powder over the top of the cake and commence stress relief.(If you are very stressed, eat with ice cream or sour cream as well!).

CHAPTER #5

5
How you can use laughter to breed success

In this chapter I give you the tools to make your life better using laughter, and to put the Happy Lemons philosophy into practice. You can try doing one of these exercises each day for an intensive course to kick start your laughter or you can take them at your own pace. My aim with this chapter is to get you on the road back to your laughing self.

Once you are in touch with your laughing self, and your laughter is free to flourish, you will find that you are better able to use laughter to connect with others, to cope with difficulties in your life, and to manage stress and tension.

Take this quiz at the beginning and end of working through this chapter, so you can track the progress you are making at freeing your laughing self, and accessing all the incredible mental and physical health benefits of laughter.

Quiz: How in touch are you with your laughing self?

Answer the following questions as honestly as you can, selecting the answer closest to how you feel, and then add up your score to find out how in touch you are with your own pure source of laughter.

You can take the quiz online at www.pinetribe.com/thomas-flindt/laughter-quiz

1. Do you feel like you behave in the same way depending on which group of people you are with? (i.e. your colleagues, friends, family or partner.)

    a) I am pretty much the same with everyone. *(score 0)*
    b) Sometimes, but sometimes I have a different persona I use with different people. *(score 1)*
    c) I feel like I am a total chameleon and that I change for every group of people in my life. *(score 2)*

2. Do you feel like your behaviour in your day-to-day life is representative of the person you feel you are on the inside?

    a) Totally – I feel like I'm living the real me. *(score 0)*
    b) Some of the time, but other times I feel like I'm not really being myself. *(score 1)*
    c) I feel like I never get to act like the real me OR I don't want to show people the real me as I don't think they'll like me. *(score 2)*

3. Do you feel that as a person, you are good enough as you are, or do you think you need to improve yourself before you can be content with yourself?

    a) I am happy with myself, I know I'm not perfect but I accept my flaws and definitely think I'm good enough. *(score 0)*

b) I think I'm OK, but I think I still need to work on myself. *(score 1)*
c) I don't think there's anything about me that doesn't need improving. *(score 2)*

4. Do your moods tend to:

a) Be quite balanced and constant, with occasional storms or floods. *(score 0)*
b) Fluctuate a bit but mostly you think it's within normal limits. *(score 1)*
c) Constantly fluctuate, you sometimes feel like you're going mad as you don't know what's coming next OR you don't really feel like you have emotions as you just feel numb. *(score 2)*

5. Do you feel like you are able to be honest with yourself about what you are feeling at any given time?

a) I'm pretty good at recognising how I feel and what I need emotionally, even when it scares or upsets me. *(score 0)*
b) I try but sometimes it's easier for me to suppress difficult or complicated feelings. *(score 1)*
c) I don't like to think about my feelings, I think it's better if I don't start stirring up that stuff. *(score 2)*

6. Do you feel like you are able to be honest with other people about what you are feeling at any given time?

a) Obviously it's not always possible, but I think it's important to be as open as I can about what's going on with me. *(score 0)*
b) Sometimes – I don't really like people to know what's going on inside that much. *(score 1)*
c) My feelings are nobody's business. *(score 2)*

7. If someone treats you badly, is your first response:

a) To feel that it's not right for them to treat you that way – you deserve better. *(score 0)*
b) To feel upset, and wonder why they treated you like that, and if maybe you did something wrong. *(score 1)*
c) I need to stop screwing up all the time, no wonder they're angry. *(score 2)*

8. If someone treats you badly, do you feel able to tell them that it's not acceptable to treat you that way?

a) Whenever the situation permits, I do so (obviously sometimes I can't, because I'm not in a position where that's possible). *(score 0)*
b) I get up the nerve to stand up for myself when someone is behaving really badly, or I'm feeling particularly confident. *(score 1)*
c) I don't really have the confidence to tell someone off like that, and anyway, it might just be me imagining it, or I might have done something to make them behave that way. *(score 2)*

9. When was the last time you laughed out loud? (Outside of our laughter exercises.)

a) Today – I find so many things funny, and laughter just seems to spring out of me! *(score 0)*
b) In the last week – I definitely can see the funny side of things but I don't spend my time laughing at everything. *(score 1)*
c) Probably in the last month or so – I don't laugh a lot so it takes something really funny to make me laugh out loud. *(score 2)*

10. Do you feel like something bad might happen if you let go of controlling every detail of your life?

a) No, it's not possible to control everything, that's unrealistic. *(score 0)*
b) I do worry sometimes about giving up control of tasks as I don't always trust other people to do things properly. *(score 1)*

c) Yes, I need to keep tight control on things so that I know that everything is how I need it to be. *(score 2)*

11. When plans change at the last minute do you feel:

a) Fairly relaxed – that's just how things go sometimes. *(score 0)*
b) A bit tense, but things will probably turn out OK. *(score 1)*
c) Panicky and afraid that everything will turn out to be a complete disaster. *(score 2)*

12. When a problem comes up unexpectedly, do you feel:

a) Fine, you trust yourself to be able to cope with it. *(score 0)*
b) Slightly panicky but you make yourself deal with fixing it, and then mop your brow when it's sorted out. *(score 1)*
c) Paralysed and defeated. *(score 2)*

13. Do you tend to worry about the past or future?

a) Not really. *(score 0)*
b) Sometimes. *(score 1)*
c) Constantly. *(score 2)*

14. Do you feel like you have enough emotional and mental energy to cope with your life, and to nurture and support your friends and family?

a) Yes, most of the time I feel like I have plenty of extra energy to give to other people as well as myself. *(score 0)*
b) Most of the time I feel like I can cope with life but often I don't have anything spare to give to others. *(score 1)*
c) I really can't handle people making emotional demands of me at the moment. I am using all my energy struggling to cope with my own life. *(score 2)*

15. How does the thought of trying something new in life (a new activity, going to a new place, meeting new people) make you feel?

    a) Excited and eager. *(score 0)*
    b) Tentatively interested – you like to push your comfort zone, but not all the time as you haven't the energy. *(score 1)*
    c) Scared and/or exhausted at the thought. *(score 2)*

16. Do you feel hopeful about your life?

    a) Oh yes! I have such big plans, and I'm so excited about the great things ahead. *(score 0)*
    b) I don't think I'm magic or anything, but I generally feel that things are going to turn out OK for me. *(score 1)*
    c) I just can't see anything positive in my future, or any hope for things to improve. *(score 2)*

17. Do you feel like you have the power to change your life to make it how you want it?

    a) Definitely – I think by taking practical steps I can achieve my dreams. *(score 0)*
    b) Sometimes / most of the time I think I can be unrealistic about what I can achieve. *(score 1)*
    c) No, I don't think my life can be different, this is what it's like, and I'm stuck with it. *(score 2)*

18. Does worrying about what other people might think of your behaviour often prevent you from doing things that make you happy?

    a) Not really, as long as I am not doing anything horrible or offensive to anyone! *(score 0)*
    b) Sometimes I don't feel confident enough to do what I really want because I worry people will think I'm stupid. *(score 1)*
    c) I'm always worried about whether people are looking at me and what they will think – it really limits what I can do in my life. *(score 2)*

19. Do you have difficulty making decisions because you doubt yourself or don't feel confident in your ability to decide?

a) Not really, I have confidence in my ability to make a good decision – and anyway, any decision is better than no decision! *(score 0)*
b) Sometimes – I worry about making the wrong decision and causing problems or getting blamed. *(score 1)*
c) All the time – I feel helpless and paralysed when I have to make a decision. *(score 2)*

20. Do you second-guess your own decisions after making them?

a) Nope – what's done is done, and if it was the wrong decision I'll just have to deal with that. *(score 0)*
b) Sometimes, if it was a decision that was really hard to make, or if I think the consequences of being wrong will be really bad. *(score 1)*
c) All the time, I'm terrified of messing up AND/OR getting in trouble. *(score 2)*

21. Do you often criticise yourself?

a) Not really, I try to admit when I'm wrong but I don't think there's any point beating yourself up about it. *(score 0)*
b) Quite often, I feel like I mess up quite a lot. *(score 1)*
c) Constantly, I never seem to be able to do anything right. *(score 2)*

22. Do you find other people very annoying?

a) Not really, I try to understand why people are the way they are and let them get on with doing things their own way. *(score 0)*
b) Sometimes, particularly when I'm in a bad mood. *(score 1)*
c) All the time, other people never seem to live up to my standards. *(score 2)*

23. Do you feel you are a good and valuable person?

a) Definitely. *(score 0)*
b) Most or some of the time, although sometimes I feel disappointed with myself or worthless. *(score 1)*
c) I feel like I am worthless or a bad person most of the time. *(score 2)*

24. Are you OK with being wrong, or having to re-evaluate your ideas or beliefs based on new perspectives?

a) Mostly, yeah. I don't know everything and that's OK. *(score 0)*
b) Sometimes, but sometimes it makes me feel small and stupid to be wrong, so I can get a bit defensive. *(score 1)*
c) I'm never wrong! OR I hate being wrong! I will never admit it publicly. *(score 2)*

Score

33 – 48 points

Your laughing self has been squashed way down inside of you by life's knocks – but don't worry, it isn't gone, it's just hiding, and this chapter can help you bring it back up into the sunshine!

Please be aware that while this course should still be able to help you feel better about yourself and about life, it is not intended as a substitute for medical treatment. If you feel you might be experiencing symptoms of depression or anxiety, please contact your doctor.

Remember, ill mental health is nothing to be ashamed or afraid of – we all get sick sometimes.

16 – 32 points

You haven't totally forgotten your laughing self, but like old friends that care about each other but don't stay in touch enough, you don't let it into your day to day life as often as you could. Follow the exercises in this chapter and your contact with your laughing self will soon be like it was the day you first laughed!

0 - 15 points
You are firmly in contact with your innocent, childlike laughing self – you take joy in your life and you are open to new people and experiences, while being honest about your authentic self. You are so lucky, well done! But don't ever neglect your laughing self or you could fall out of touch and lose the sparkle from your life.

Getting in touch with your laughing self

The laughter list

Make a laughter list. On this list, write down five to ten things that make you laugh (although you don't have to stop at ten!). This might be TV shows, films, games, stupid videos on the internet, pets or people you know. If you want more laughter in your life, be aware of where the sources of laughter lie.

Put this list up somewhere you can see it, and look at it every day.

Get stimulated

> Every child is an artist. The problem is how to remain an artist when you become an adult.
>
> *- Pablo Picasso*

Art

It is paradoxical that we adults pay so much attention to the sensory stimulation of our children, yet we forget it ourselves. Crèches, kindergartens and schools all know that it is important for children to experience every dimension of the senses. Art and crafts, music, sport, playtime, dance, imagination and storytelling are thus a completely natural part of any day for a child in a crèche, kindergarten or school. Why? Because it is important for balanced development. As we never, ever stop developing until the day we die, there will be parts of us that will be under stimulated if we do not utilise all our senses throughout life.

In Denmark, all children study art and crafts as an integral part of their school timetable. All children should have the chance to work with their creativity. Drawing, painting or sculpting is a fantastic way of expressing oneself, especially for those children who are not able to express themselves through their body or through words. To draw and paint can open up deeper levels of understanding and creativity, just as it allows a free channel for the expression of our subconscious selves.

Occasionally, the established art world has a shock for the public. In Denmark, for example, it was once revealed that Vitus, the artist responsible for a successful exhibition at a reputable art gallery, was actually only three years old! The art critics, oblivious to the artist's true identity, praised his work in golden tones.

Yet for me, art is not reserved for a particular age group, it has no set form and should not be subject to limitation; it's the chance to sidestep all convention and explore our unlimited possibility for expression. Use this endless possibility and let yourself create.

A Colourful Exercise

Visit your local art shop and buy a set of paints, some paper and some paintbrushes. Go somewhere peaceful, either at home or outdoors. Then imagine you are three years old, and paint a picture. (You don't have to use the paintbrushes, you can use your hands!) Let your imagination flow!

Music

The amusement and enthusiasm I felt on first hearing the term, 'Laughter Club' was very similar to the way I felt when I saw a TV feature about a singing group for the tone deaf. Thirty or forty people gathered in a circle, singing their hearts out in a blend of bass, soprano and tenor – completely and utterly out of tune. Indomitable, joyful singers, who refused to let themselves be intimidated by the sweet and velvet voices of standard pop. In this club, there were no holds barred when it came to song. You could just see that the more out of tune they sung, the happier they seemed to be – fantastic!

Song opens the body on many levels. Laughter is also about opening the body and mind. A good exercise to bring more laughter into your life is to begin to sing more in your everyday life. For example, sing along with your favourite songs when you listen to the radio.

All forms of playing with language, sound and song will open up your creativity and help you get closer to your laughing self. The more you play with your creative expression, the more easily it will spontaneously flow from you.

Exercise: Dundadada dun dun

Think of one of your current favourite songs and turn it into a 'hum-dinger'. You could also hum, 'da-di-da' and 'la-la-la' to a TV programme's theme tune. For example, you could try the theme-tune from Dallas - you know! - the TV series from the 80's with JR and Bobby Ewing, Sue Ellen and the rest of them. I think it went something like this:

da dummmmm da dummmmm da daaa dadaadaa
daaa daaa daaa daa dum dum dummmmm
da daaa daaa daaa deedee dumm deedee dumm dumm
daaaa diddy daaaaa daaa diiiiiiiiiiiiiiiiii

Use your imagination

Children have a highly developed imagination. Imagination is not just 'fiction'. For a child, imagination is a big part of the whole experience of life. If you have had to put imagination to one side as an adult, you now have the choice to bring it back into your life again. (Although I definitely don't mean that you should dress up as Superman and jump from a tall building.)

We base our idea of what is possible from experience, but we should be basing it on imagination – this allows us to see that our life can be how we want it to be, even if our life so far has not shown us this possibility. You can get closer to the life you dreamed about as a child, or that you dream of here and now as an adult. You can actually begin today. It all starts with your imagination.

Thought a Action a Reality

Exercise: Focus on your wildest dreams

Sit down and let your thoughts flow freely. Write down your greatest vision and your heartfelt wishes. Write down your wildest dreams. Describe your life's most wonderful adventure. You are just a step away from making it a reality.

In your wildest dreams, where do you wake up in the morning? What kind of mood are you in? Who do you say good morning to? Describe your dream woman or your dream man (if you haven't already met them!), or your dream family. What does your home look like? Describe it room by room. Describe the atmosphere in this home, the views from the windows, the neighbours, the town it is situated in. Where do you work? What do you do? How much money do you earn? What makes your job satisfying? What contribution are you making to the world? How happy are you and how happy are the people around you?

Try and make a list of ways in which you could get closer to this using small practical steps.

It is said that good luck arises when chance and good preparation meet each other. When you are able to feel how your dream life actually feels, then you are also ready to take action when an opportunity to follow your dream appears.

Move

The body is in the present moment. It is the mind that, for some reason or other, is always trying to run away into the future or the past. Children are much more at home in their bodies than we adults are. As children, life is experienced in the body, but when we become adults, we move up into our heads, so that life is experienced more on the mental level. Life becomes more thought than felt.

As a child, you found it easy to move your body - there were no concepts of 'right' or 'wrong' movement. In other words, the body of a child is free to follow its own will to move and feel. Our body and mind are part of the same self, but we often stop using our bodies so joyfully as we become older, and close down part of our laughing self. You must use your fantastic, flexible body. The body needs a great deal of movement, including creative movement. It's not enough just to go down to the corner shop every day. I want to encourage you to explore more imaginative and celebratory ways in which your body can move.

Exercise: Ministry of silly walks

Have you ever seen the Monty Python sketch, Ministry of Silly Walks? (If not, you can watch it here: www.pinetribe.com/thomas-flindt/silly-walk)
In it, all the characters walk around in strange and wacky ways.
Come up with your own silly walk – as simple or as complicated as you

like - but make sure it's completely ridiculous and miles away from your normal walk. Exaggerate your arm or leg movements. Lift your legs a bit too high or add a little cha-cha-cha to your arm movements. You could also add a little dance number to it if you wanted.

Try this on your own to start with. (Although it can be really fun to do with other people!) Spend ten minutes around the house doing your normal tasks but doing your silly walk as well.

Sport should not just be experienced on the TV, but also in reality, preferably a few times a week. When we exercise, we 'ground' ourselves in our bodies. It is just as important for us to exercise our bodies as it is for us to exercise our minds. As adults we should remember, that we don't have a body – we are a body! Your body is you, the biggest part of you. If your body is under stimulated, then you are under stimulated. When you play sport, and I don't mean darts or billiards here, but something that gets your pulse racing, you set your body free. Your body relaxes and lets go when you exercise, both physically and mentally.

If you have ever jogged, cycled or swum regularly, then I am sure you will agree that after exercising, your mind feels significantly lighter. The energy you invest will return to you tenfold. Thus, if you work out for three hours a week, you can count on at least 30 hours of vital, new energy in return for your investment. The medical profession seems also to have got the message, with more and more doctors now prescribing exercise for their patients. Preventative medicine is always the best medicine.

Exercise: Exercise!

If you are already exercising vigorously for an hour, three times a week then congratulations, you're doing enough to help keep your body and mind healthy! (But even more would be great, and would make you feel fantastic!)

If you're not, don't despair – you may have been put off sport from bad experiences at school (we've all been there), you may have difficulty making time for it because of your responsibilities, or you may find it difficult to exercise because of your health or your weight. Almost everyone can find a way of exercising that works for them. (It might not be possible if you're disabled or chronically ill.)

Make a list (this is where we use our imagination again) of all the different kinds of sport you can think of. You might want to use the internet to look up some really weird ones. Once you've got at least thirty on there, pick out the one you think looks the most fun.

If it's something totally impossible (like camel riding when you live in Scotland) then try and see what the nearest you can come to it is, and make an appointment to try it (maybe you could try horse-riding instead?).

You can find ways to get cheap deals online for loads of sports. See if you can drag some friends along too! You could try one new type of exercise per month until you find one that you really love – it's much easier to make time in your life for something if it brings you pure joy and makes you feel incredible.

Play

> We don't stop playing because we grow old,
> We grow old because we stop playing.
> - *George Bernard Shaw*

Play is the natural way to explore our creativity, but we stop doing it as we get older. Anything is possible in the world of play – isn't that a liberating thought? We can bring this freedom into our daily lives by opening ourselves up using the creativity of play.

Many of the greatest artists and inventors throughout history were amazingly good at playing. If you entertain the thought that anything is possible, then you open the door to creativity.

Therefore, it is also important that you, as an adult, stimulate your brain through playful activity. You express and develop yourself both consciously and unconsciously when you play. When we adults deal with our daily tasks and working life, we usually operate within the framework of what we believe is possible. Remember, it is only the sum of your previous experiences that provides the framework of what you believe is possible for you. When we bring play to our daily tasks and objectives, we will suddenly notice things we didn't think were possible. There is a coupling between play and practicality that leads to the development of new skills and ideas.

Exercise: Problem-solving via play

Next time you come across a problem (whether in your private life or at work), use play to solve it.

First, replace the word 'problem' with 'challenge'. If you become frightened or overwhelmed, you will have trouble acting to solve it.

Then take a step back, and imagine you are one of history's great artists. Playfully open up for a creative flow of ideas and thoughts. Play that anything is possible. Play that there are no limitations. Play that your ideas will change the course of history itself. (Maybe they will!)

It is also healthy to play when you need a break from yourself or your work. If your brain has been working under great pressure for a long time, then it needs a break to play. Many companies have found out how important this need is. In my work as a laughter leader, I have visited hundreds of businesses over the past decade, and have noticed that those workplaces characterised by a particular enthusiasm and energy amongst employees, were those where management had an explicit policy recognising the importance of play at work. Table tennis, go-carts, table football and all kinds of other toys were made freely available to the employees.

Fantastic! But also pretty much common sense. A fun, happy and playful worker must be preferable to the opposite. In reality, it is not really children who need more toys, but us adults. When will Toys 'R' Us open a department for 18-90 year olds? I'm serious. So if you work for Toys 'R' Us please take this challenge up immediately.

Exercise: Fake it till you make it

This is another fun way to attack your problems and your fears using play. If you want to excel at something, pretend to yourself that you already excel.

When I first starting working with people through laughter, I had to do lots of things that were outside of my comfort zone, so I used play to help me. When I had to ring up lots of companies to offer them courses, I found it quite scary and difficult. So I tried a completely different tactic. I played that I was ringing people up. I imagined that the people who answered the telephone when I rang were not really serious business folk, but just 'stand-ins' I could practise on. Imagining that I was already an expert at this, and that the other people were not intimidating, helped me relax and learn to use the skills I already had to get a handle on what I was doing.

Try doing this next time you have to tackle a task that intimidates you.

Happy adults are really just happy children, who have grown a little older. Many happy adults allow themselves to just enjoy and experience life as children do. The child that is our laughing self is within us all. If you forget to look after or play with this child, you are forgetting an essential aspect of your life. Indeed, laughter often arises and manifests through playfulness and the experience and release of creativity.

Exercise: Talk nonsense

Persuade a friend to help you with this exercise. Try and have a conversation with them for five minutes using your normal expressions and tone of voice, but using completely nonsense words.

Children laugh much more freely than adults, so we can learn from them how to get back in touch with our laughing selves. If you have children, then play with them, learn from them. If you don't have children, then borrow some from friends or family. Spend time with children and learn how simple it is to enjoy life. Learn to play, to use your imagination, to dance crazily, to be taken by laughter and to use language freely and without worries. Make faces, do handstands, listen to music and sing along wildly. Let yourself go and experience that you are weightless and free. Release your laughing self and laugh with everything you are.

Let go of perfectionism

For many years of my life, I was strongly influenced by the assumption that I had to be perfect. It almost hurts to write this now, because I am reminded of a very inhibited and uncomfortable period of my life. Thankfully, I managed to create some mess-ups during this period, but generally, I was controlled by the belief that I had to say the right thing, do the right thing and look the right way. You can probably imagine how such an approach to life can block one's authentic laughing self from emerging. Laughter is about loosening up and it is extremely hard to do this if you are holding on tightly to a particular self-image. My 'perfect' period can in no way be described as one characterised by laughter and the joy of life.

The first step towards my 'perfect life' was to let go of the idea that I had to be perfect. I have now introduced the 80/20 rule into my life. This rule means that it is OK to be 'perfect' at what I am doing, both privately and professionally, around 80% of the time. And it is OK for me to be less perfect or to make mistakes around 20% of the time.

This 80/20 rule has simply made my life easier.

Exercise: The 80/20 rule in action

Apply the 80/20 rule in your life for a week and see how it works for you.

Sometimes when we set new goals in life, we put so much pressure on ourselves that we make it more difficult to succeed. You have probably tried in the past to lose weight, stop smoking or start exercising. Going for a 100 percent success rate will work for very few people. For most people, starting a new challenge in such a perfectionist way is setting themselves up for failure.

If you are trying to change your habits right now, or if you have a tendency to be very hard on yourself – practise being kind to yourself this week by cutting yourself slack 20% of the time. You will see that you can take the pressure off yourself, and still achieve the same (or better!) results.

Positive Affirmations

The mind needs nourishment just like the body does. Write out the following list and place it somewhere where you will see it every day.

The truth about life

You are unique.
You are one of a kind.
You are loved just as you are.
You have unlimited possibilities in this life.
You contain everything within you
to create success.
You are truth.
You are will power.
You are limitless possibility.
You are completely special.
You are the creator of your own life.
Use your life – use yourself.

Track your progress

So, how does it feel?

Do you feel your laughter bubbling up more easily? Is it becoming easier to access the natural joy inside you?

Take the quiz 'How in touch are you with your laughing self?' again to track your progress in reaching your childlike laughing self.

You can take the quiz online at www.pinetribe.com/thomas-flindt/laughter-quiz

I hope that reading this book is the beginning of a beautiful journey for you, down a road full of love and laughter, where you take charge of the destination and where every day brings you fresh happiness. Remember that a really great day starts with a good night's sleep.

Exercise: The recipe for a really good night's sleep

Half an hour before you go to bed in the evening, take out your diary. I recommend a big A5 one.

Open your diary at tomorrow's date.
Write down all your goals and tasks for the day.
Write down everything that you can think of that you wish to complete tomorrow.
In this way, you can let go of all thoughts about the future and instead focus on what you have to do right now: Sleep!
Tomorrow is all done and dusted.

Now open your diary up at today's date and write down five of the day's absolute high points.

They can be small or large positive events or experiences you had. For example:

- an unexpected smile from a stranger on the street
- positive feedback or a compliment from a colleague
- a helping hand you gave today
- a phone call from a good friend
- a beautiful sky over your town

Lay your head on your pillow, close your eyes and visualise the good experiences you had today.

Good night and sleep well!

Love from Thomas the Laughter Guru

CHAPTER #6

6
Exercises

Extra laughter exercises

If you have already tried arranging a group laughter session in your own home, and you have been bitten by the crazy laughing bug, here are some additional laughter exercises for you to try that have arisen within laughter circles over the years. Many of these exercises are used the world over. They are probably instructed and executed in the same way in Spain as they are in Greenland (remember, humour is cultural, laughter is universal!). However, do remember that you are perfectly entitled to give an exercise your own special touch - if you happen to find an angle which makes it funnier in some way, then go for it. Let your imagination run wild! Most laughter exercises are of Indian origin. But the possibilities are endless.

Mobile phone laughter

Pretend you have a mobile phone in your hand and hold it up to your ear. The telephone is your clenched fist, with your little finger as the mouthpiece and your thumb as the antenna. Imagine that you are listening to something incredibly funny. Initiate the exercise and tell the group to move around amongst each other while they laugh hysterically at what they are hearing. You can also listen to each other's 'mobiles'.

The laughter of equality

In this exercise, we bring equality of the sexes into the laughter, with women laughing like men and men laughing like women. If you are a man taking on a feminine laugh, then really over-emphasise your feminine mannerisms. Let yourself be silly - move your hands in an overtly feminine way and laugh loudly but in a light tone of voice. Likewise, if you are a women laughing like a man, then over-do the masculine gestures and the deep voice. Puff yourself up a bit and walk round jovially thumping each other on the back.

Thigh-slapping laughter

Slap your thighs, one after the other, while laughing. Find a rhythm where the slaps beat in time with your laughter. You can also slap your neighbour's thighs. The winner is the one with the reddest thighs…

The laugh-crying exercise

This is one of my favourite exercises. Here, you laugh and cry simultaneously. Stand in a circle. Demonstrate the exercise by putting your hands to your eyes and pretending to cry while slowly bending over. Cry the whole way down, holding your hands up to your eyes until you reach your knees. When you reach your knees, stretch out your arms and laugh the entire way back up again. Do this exercise up to three times and stretch out afterwards.

Pay cheque laughter

This exercise was devised by a guy called Steen. I once facilitated 14 days of morning laughter with a company called Guideix. Steen, who worked for this company, thought that the size of the salary that was transferred to his bank account each month was pretty laughable.

This is a really fun exercise to do. Use the palm of your outstretched hand to represent a piece of paper. Turn the palm of your hand upwards and walk around pointing at the palm of your hand as if it were a paycheque. With a chortle and guffaw, show each other the ridiculously low figure on the cheque.

Slow motion laughter

On TV, they sometimes show things in slow motion. Everything moves very slowly and there is not a sound to be heard. We do exactly the same thing with slow motion laughter. Walk or run around slowly amongst each other, laughing very slowly and silently.

Drunken laughter

Imagine you have a full bottle of laughter in your hand and you are already a bit tipsy from its delightful effects. Take a swig from the bottle, hiccup and take a little jump. How wonderful to be so merrily drunk on pure laughter. Reel and sway as you move around amongst each other.

REFERENCES

1. In May 2007, *Four Systems* was acquired by one of Denmark's largest IT companies, I2I – www.i2i.dk

2. Taken from "Laugh for No Reason" by Dr Madan Kataria, Madhuri International, 1999

3. From an interview with Patch Adams: www.youtube.com/watch?v=SARHCS8DRJE

4. From a lecture by Patch Adams: www.youtube.com/watch?v=Maw4Xg-6RAw

5. www.bowlingalone.gom

6. http://www.cohesioninstitute.org.uk/Resources/Toolkits/Health/HealthAndCommunityCohesion/AContributorToHealth

7. www.livescience.com/6946-joke-animals-laugh.html

8. greatergood.berkeley.edu/article/item/why_laughter_is_contagious

9. Rankin, A.M.; Philip, P.J. (May 1963). "An epidemic of laughing in the Bukoba district of Tanganyika". Central African Journal of Medicine 9: 167–170. PMID 13973013.

10. www.psychologicalscience.org/index.php/news/releases/smiling-facilitates-stress-recovery.html

11. Willumsen, Skamris, Hedegaard, Sørensen & Witek, (2005), "Laughter clubs", Faculty of Social Sciences, Institute of Anthropology, Copenhagen University.

12. www.bbc.co.uk/science/humanbody/mind/surveys/smiles/index_22.shtml

13. Article by Dr Stephen Diamond www.psychologytoday.com/blog/evil-deeds/201204/essential-secrets-psychotherapy-what-is-the-shadow

14. Neuroendocrine perspectives on social attachment and love www.ncbi.nlm.nih.gov/pubmed/9924738

15. Inspired by "Heartache Chocolate Cake" by Harry Eastwood, from the cookbook Red Velvet Chocolate Heartache, Bantam Press, 2009.

Lightning Source UK Ltd.
Milton Keynes UK
UKOW01f0330280817
308040UK00002B/50/P